Software Engineering for Micros

The Electrifying Streamlined Blueprint Speedcode Method

Hayden Computer Programming Series

Software Engineering for Micros

The Electrifying Streamlined Blueprint Speedcode Method

T. G. LEWIS

Associate Professor
Department of Computer Science
Oregon State University

HAYDEN BOOK COMPANY, INC.
Rochelle Park, New Jersey

To Madeline
Appellation Controlee 1949

Library of Congress Cataloging in Publication Data

Lewis, Theodore Gyle
  Software engineering for micros.

  (Hayden computer programming series)
  Includes index.
  1. Microcomputers—Programming. 2. Microprocessors—
Programming. I. Title.
QA76.6.L48   001.6'4'04   79-19222
ISBN 0-8104-5166-2

| 1 | 2 | 3 | 4 | 5 | 6 | 7 | 8 | 9 | PRINTING |

| 79 | 80 | 81 | 82 | 83 | 84 | 85 | 86 | 87 | YEAR |

Preface

Not long ago, giant computing machines roamed the corporations, universities, and governmental departments. They were magnificent, with expansive arrays of flashing lights, fantastic electromechanical devices for moving tapes and disks, line printers, and other miscellaneous peripheral units. In those not-too-distant days gone by, the **machine** was the **system**.

Visitors to our computer center are increasingly blasé about their field trip. Nowadays computers simply fail to hold the attention of on-lookers. There are few big boxes, flashing displays, and moving parts. Quite simply, hardware has shrunk to its vanishing point. In a modern computer the **software** is the **system**. And onlookers cannot see software.

The microprocessor revolution happened too quickly. There are few proven rules, established facts, ready solutions, or easy answers. About the only things we have to go by are two suspicions: • Software is going to continue to be a larger part of the total cost of a computer system • The microprocessor revolution is a rapid reinvention of the third-generation computer era, only this time the cost functions are different.

By emphasizing the cost of software and rephrasing the development of third-generation computing in modern terms, we can gain insight into the effects of the microprocessor revolution: Batch systems will be replaced by stand-alone "personal" computing systems operated by their owners. Assembly languages appeared early and will rapidly die out in favor of system implementation languages. Timesharing is supplanted by datasharing (multiple processor access to a shared storage space). Large hardware systems become large software systems in a small box. Multiprogramming gives way to networking.

There are problems. Multiple processor systems imply a complexity of their own. And then there are problems: The computer industry is shifting to more difficult applications. Hence, the complexity of systems is increasing, generally. The keyword here is **complexity**. Exactly how are programmers of the 1980s going to cope with complexity? By understanding the increasingly important field of software engineering.

Software engineering is the discipline of designing, implementing, testing, and certifying software systems. It is eclectic, dynamic, and difficult. It encompasses techniques developed in the last 10 years, techniques developed last year, and techniques currently being developed.

The purpose of this book is to get you started. Each chapter is a statement of a software engineering concept. The text fleshes-out concepts and illustrates their manifestation in the microcomputer world.

This material has been used in sophomore computer science courses; specifically, in a microcomputer laboratory. The strict adherents to the Electrifying Streamlined Blueprint Speedcode Method consider the course easy. The undisciplined undergraduate who fails to take the time to exercise this method has difficulty with the course. Enough said.

I owe much to those who contributed. Mrs. Clara Homyer typed the original, Henry Ledgard made valuable comments, and Dianne Littwin had the daring to publish this.

T. G. LEWIS

Corvallis, Oregon

Contents

Software Engineering for Micros

for Micros

*The Electrifying Streamlined
Blueprint Speedcode Method*

1

Million Dollar Programs, Ten Dollar Computers

Three days passed before Stravinski Codeov whirled out of his cata-tonic trance and feverishly sprayed code onto his assembly language coding forms. For days he labored over the new program, never looking up or leaving his desk. The midnight janitors were careful to mop around Codeov's feet while he perspired under the intense light of a tensor lamp. His fellow programmers avoided him, awaiting the inevitable day when Stravinski would slump forward over his completed duty, banging his forehead on the desk top. His supervisor would then extricate the stack of coding forms from beneath Codeov's wearied body and send them off to Keypunching.

Stravinski Codeov was an eccentric superprogrammer, not unlike thousands of others. Held in awe by his co-workers, he averaged hun-dreds of lines of near-flawless code per day.

One day Codeov stopped working, and the familiar thump of cra-nium impacting desk top was not heard. Silence boomed throughout the Data Processing Department, and inquisitive heads raised to see what had happened. Codeov stood up, put on his coat, hat, and imported racing gloves, and walked out the door. Stravinski Codeov was burned out.

* * *

Superprogrammer Stumbles

Able to leap a tall CPU, speedily code past the fastest line printer, sweep keypunch operators off their feet with a single line of elegant Fortran—these are the abilities of a superprogrammer. The rampant notoriety of superprogrammers needs no help from innocent bystanders. Everyone involved with the microprocessor renaissance is enviously aware of their talents. We who do not possess such superhuman powers often wonder what it takes to be a superprogrammer. However, the superpro-grammer tale is often linked with a tortoise and hare story. An example will clarify this relationship.

Peter Plodder is slow, methodical, and very meticulous. A mild-mannered, quiet person (with good taste in clothes), he had the irritating habit of issuing long project completion times to his supervisor. Blustering Barton, on the other hand, was a flashy, outspoken superprogrammer who consistently completed his programming assignments ahead of the most optimistic estimates.

The Software Division management loved Blust, but hardly knew Peter was alive. Consequently, Blust was granted a six-month leave of absence—a biscuit for his programming accomplishments. A temporary programmer was hired to maintain Blust's code while he was away.

Six weeks after Barton embarked on a plane for Africa, his payroll system program failed. The substitute programmer immediately plunged into Barton's program to try to isolate the bug. Perhaps not so surprisingly, he was never able to break into the code. In Blustering Barton's race to produce code, he neglected to write easy-to-understand programs, and his documentation was a mess. In short, only Barton himself could repair the programs he had written.

Meanwhile, back at the desk of Peter Plodder business was progressing as usual. Organization and clearly documented programs were his trademark. In fact, Peter was called on to try to find the bug in Barton's payroll program. His time estimate for the debugging task was customarily protracted, but the management had no choice. With Blustering Barton away and the temporary programmer stymied, they had to go with Peter.

Eventually the bug was located and corrected, but everyone knew the superprogrammer had stumbled. Summarily, new programming standards were implemented. Peter was invited to teach the other programmers how to write readable code. He showed everyone (including Blustering Barton, when he returned) how to make programs self-documenting. His methodology was adopted as the only acceptable methodology to be used throughout the Software Division.

*　　　*　　　*

Programming is a labor-intensive manufacturing process. Billions of dollars are spent each year on software system maintenance. Consequently, in an effort to reduce the cost of program development, large and small companies alike have adopted a variety of labor-saving methodologies. One such methodology is proposed in this book.

The Electrifying, Blueprint Speedcode Method is presented here, but there are other methodologies that result in improved programmer productivity: structured design, composite design, blueprint design. But these methodologies and their corresponding rules for properly structured programs are *not religions*. They are simply various manifestations of a *disciplined approach to writing reliable programs.*

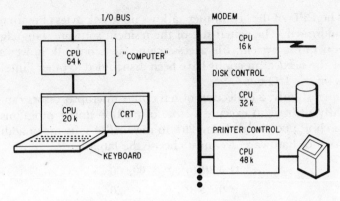

Fig. 1.1   A distributed microcomputer system.

Cost reductions are realized when a particular discipline becomes rote to the human programmer. At first, this discipline may appear to be too time-consuming and repetitious. Don't be misled by this initial impression. Remember, the total cost of software production is the sum of design, implementation, testing, and maintenance costs. In the final analysis, discipline will produce software at a lower total cost than any undisciplined methodology.

Presently, microcomputer programmers live in a strange world of economic anomaly. The cost of hardware has diminished to the point where we must alter our goals.

The Memory Myth. Programs should be kept compact due to the high cost of memory.

Fact. Memory is "free," but addressability is a bottleneck. Therefore, it may be necessary to distribute programs over several microprocessors, each with a certain maximum amount of memory addressability (usually 64k).

The memory myth is concerned with program size and memory costs. The actual cost of semiconductor memory is relatively low, especially when compared with the cost of filling memory with programs. The *address space* of most microprocessors is, as previously mentioned, limited to 64k however, and this is a problem. One solution is to include several microprocessors in a system in order to increase the memory space available for resident programs.

As an example of the memory myth solution, let's consider a computer system incorporating a keyboard, CRT display, disk drives, and telecommunications modem. Such an assemblage is depicted in Fig. 1.1. The memory space of this distributed microprocessor system totals 180k —considerably more than the addressability of most single-microprocessor systems.

The CPU of the "computer" allows up to 64k bytes of main memory to be addressed. The actual size of the resident software (language processor, operating system, file access methods) is only 4k however, since most of the needed functions have been distributed to other "intelligent" devices on the I/O bus.

Interestingly, a collection of ten dollar microprocessors can be economically utilized to execute a store of million dollar programs. Now, given a choice between adding 20% to the cost of software or adding 20% to the cost of hardware, we must choose the latter.

$$0.2(\$10^6) = \$200,000$$
$$0.2(\$10^2) = \quad \$20$$

Clearly, one way to reduce the overall cost of a hardware–software system is to shift some tasks from software to hardware. We advocate this approach of reducing labor-intensive programming tasks by allowing "less efficient" programs (that is, programs that require more memory).

Program Efficiency Myth. An efficient program is a tightly compacted string of code that takes advantage of every machine feature to reduce the number of instructions in the program.

Fact. An efficient program is a string of code that is easy to implement, easy to understand, and therefore reliable. It is easy to maintain, but may be larger than the minimum size possible.

In the next section we develop a software engineering approach to programming microprocessors.

The Secret Recipe of Speedcode

Software engineering is the discipline of structured design, structured coding, structured testing, and structured documentation. Obviously, the notion of structure plays a dominant role in software engineering.

Structuralism can have a big impact on programming and software production. It can reduce costs by reducing the time it takes to code a program. Moreover, the resulting software runs sooner, is initially correct, and remains correct after years of use. The full impact of structuralism is revealed by the savings enjoyed when an old program is maintained by a programmer who had nothing to do with the original implementation.

We can illustrate structuralism by considering the job of a structural (civil) engineer. Suppose a new building is to be constructed. First, an overall plan is made by an architect for the buyer to see. This plan includes the functional specifications of the building. That is, it will depict an office, garage, school, or some other structure. The artist's rendition of the finished building is most valuable to the buyer. But since it uses levels of abstraction to "hide" details the buyer is not concerned with, it is useless to the building contractor. More detailed abstractions of the building are required by the contractor, and these are provided by floor plans, heating plans, electrical plans, mason's plans, etc. Finally, the actual construction of the building takes place in steps, and each step is specified in advance. Thus, lumber is not needed for the walls until the foundation is poured, and so on.

The design of a new building is an engineering task. The design of a computer program is also an engineering task. Thus, we need a methodology that will guarantee success. The keystones of structuralism are:

1. Planning
2. Levels of abstraction
3. Modularity
4. Limited control structures
5. Testing early in the design

The first three steps of this methodology can be illustrated with a simple application program. Suppose we want to write a program to accept a string of input characters from a keyboard and in turn output the line to a line printer. The program must incorporate the necessary I/O routines and added frills like echoing the keystrokes to a CRT display. A carriage return CR will terminate each line of input.

First we must describe an overall plan. This plan is called the zero-level blueprint, or simply BLUE_0.

BLUE_0
1. Get characters from the keyboard.
2. Store the characters in a buffer memory.
3. Write the buffer to the line printer.
4. Take note of the CR delimiter.

end BLUE_0

Our method's second proposition specifies use of levels of abstraction in describing the program. The second-level blueprint is appropriately called BLUE_1. This level is written in *pseudocode* (a form of English) that will be refined in the next chapter.

BLUE_1
1.1 Data:
    (a) I = counter for the number of characters input.
    (b) LINE (I) = buffer array containing the input.
    (c) N = length of the line.
    (d) CR = carriage return.
    (e) CH = character input.
1.2 Input from the keyboard starting with I = 0:
    (a) CH = input.
    (b) Output CH to screen.
    (c) LINE (I) = CH.
    (d) Increment I by 1.
    (e) Exit when CH = CR or I = (N — 1).
    (f) Repeat (a) through (f).

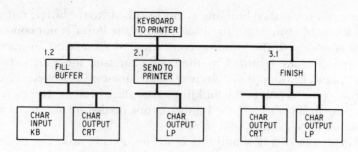

Fig. 1.2   The modules of **BLUE₁**.

2.1 Write the buffer to the printer starting with I = (N — 1):
    (a) CH = LINE (N — 1 — I).
    (b) Output CH to printer.
    (c) Decrement I by 1.
    (d) Exit when I is less than 0.
    (e) Repeat (a) through (e).
3.1 Finish:
    (a) Output a line feed to keyboard.
    (b) Output a line feed to printer.
end BLUE₁

The second blueprint is still not perfect. We could clean it up and add some aesthetic touches to it after a few more iterations, but it serves to illustrate the increase in detail inherent in the next level of abstraction. In the next chapter we will formalize the **BLUE₁** level. This will enable us to produce reliable machine code for a variety of microprocessors without the effort normally needed to write symbolic machine language programs.

The third assertion of the refinement process calls for modularity. The simple example we used provides few opportunities to modularize, but the chart of Fig. 1.2 demonstrates what can be done using modular decomposition. The solution of the problem is broken into three basic sections as indicated by modules 1.2, 2.1, and 3.1. These are further modularized by calling the I/O routines. Note the use of OUTPUT LP and OUTPUT CRT in two places. The illustration also shows how we employ *hierarchical refinement* to ease the programmer's burden.

In the next chapter we develop our theory to a greater level of sophistication and explore modular decomposition in greater detail. (Even this book is an example of software engineering using levels of abstraction.) Before doing so, however, the necessary evil we call *kludgecode* must be introduced.

Building Blocks and Kludgecode

The software engineering discipline described in the previous section does not mention the actual code produced for a specific microprocessor. In fact, it is a tribute to our methodology that a particular machine language has not been introduced during design of software. This notion is repeated in the following myth.

The Kludgecode Myth. Software design must include consideration of a particular machine architecture in order to take advantage of exceptional machine features.

Fact. Software design must be machine-independent, thus removing machine features from the design and precluding potentially un-reliable programs.

The blueprint level denoted **BLUE₁** is a pseudocode that can be formalized into a notation we call *speedcode*. The speedcode specification of a program can then be refined into a particular microprocessor assembly language called *kludgecode*. Thus, the next level of refinement, **BLUE₂,** is actually a program suitable for translation by the assembler of a given machine.

BLUE₂
      "Kludgecode for machine M."
end BLUE₂

The next level of refinement is the output from the assembler. It is binary *object code*, ready to be executed by the microcomputer.

BLUE₃
      "Binary object code for machine M."
end BLUE₃

We will use several kludgecodes to illustrate the **BLUE₂** levels in sample programs. The Motorola 6800 assembler will be used most often, with the Intel 8080 assembler notation being used occasionally to demonstrate the generality of speedcode. The Appendix contains a listing of 6800 and 8080 refinements for the speedcode building blocks used over and over again in this book.

Speedcode is amazingly simple. This is its greatest virtue. We define every data value in speedcode as one of three types:

byte
word
address

A variable is designated as such by signifying with the **var** keyword. A constant is tagged using the **const** keyword. In every case the initial value of a variable or the definition of a constant is signaled by an equate =. Some examples will serve to illustrate this notation.

```
var    ZAP    : byte
const ZIP     : byte = 10
var    COUNT : byte = 60
```

The variable ZAP is an 8-bit byte with no initial value. The value of variable COUNT is 60 initially, but since it is a variable its value may be altered during the course of computation. The value of ZIP will always be 10—it is a constant, as signified by the tag **const.**

An address can be initialized in speedcode by use of equating symbols. Whenever a symbol is to be used as an address we must indicate this by prefixing the "commercial at" symbol @. The "number" (or "pound") character # is used as a prefix to indicate that the address is to be used as opposed to the value stored in that memory location. An assignment statement is indicated by the := operator.

```
var LOCATION : address = #COUNT
            @LOCATION:= 5
```

The variable LOCATION is actually a 16-bit address initially set to the address of variable COUNT. The # prefix indicates that the address of COUNT is to be used as opposed to the value stored in COUNT. When the expression on the right-hand side is evaluated, it is stored at the location specified by LOCATION, because we have used the @ prefix. Thus, 5 is stored in COUNT. This has the same effect as

```
COUNT:= 5
```

Let us use this formalized notation to write a speedcode version of the data section of the **BLUE**$_1$ specification for the keyboard–input–printer–output problem discussed in the previous section.

```
var               I : byte
var     LINE (10) : byte
var            CH : byte
const           N : byte = 11
const          CR : byte = 13
```

The variable LINE is 11 bytes long because the array always starts at 0: LINE (0), LINE (1), . . . , LINE (10). Hence, the value of N is held constant at 11. Also, the ASCII code for a carriage return CR is the decimal integer 13.

We can modularize speedcode by wrapping the modules in a procedure notation. Thus, a module is in the format

```
NAME: procedure (LIST)
      "Body of module."
end NAME
```

The invocation of a procedure is done by issuing the name of the procedure and passing the values of parameters through the LIST in parentheses. This form of calling is familiar to programmers who use Fortran, Algol, etc.

```
INPUT: procedure (LOCATION : address)
       ____
       ____

       ____
       return
end INPUT
```

Suppose the INPUT module were written and stored in its assembled speedcode form in the program memory of a microcomputer. It is ready to be called by another module. We could invoke it as follows:

```
var PTR : address = #BUFFER
_____

_____
INPUT (PTR)
_____

_____
```

The value of PTR is the address of a memory location called BUFFER. This location will receive the input from some device.

The speedcode notation can easily be refined into microcomputer instructions and pseudo-operations. Suppose we refine the following **BLUE$_1$** speedcode into Motorola 6800 assembler notation (**BLUE$_2$**).

```
BLUE₁
        var              I : byte
        var    LINE (10) : byte
        const       CR : byte = 13
        var         PTR : address = #I
        var          Y : word
end BLUE₁
```

This code is easily refined into the pseudo-ops of FCB (form constant byte), FDB (form double byte), RMB (reserve memory byte), and EQU (equate) in 6800 assembler notation.

```
BLUE₂
    I    RMB   1     **var            : byte
    LINE RMB  11     **var LINE (10)  : byte
    CR   EQU #13     **const CR       : byte = 13
    PTR  FDB   #I    **var PTR        : address = #I
    Y    FDB   #0    **var Y          : word
end BLUE₂
```

The data management of a module is a very important part of a programmer's job. The module is useless however without action. What speedcode notations are useful and sufficient for writing the action part of programs?

The building blocks of speedcode are amazingly simple. Only three standard blocks are needed to write any program. These are executed by the microcomputer: (a) one after the other; (b) as loops; and (c) as blocks that make a decision and cause a branch down one path or another.

Such simplicity is the key to the elegance of speedcode, and also why it is so reliable. All matter in the universe is constructed from electrons, protons, and neutrons. Similarly, three building blocks form the fundamental elements of all programs, and all programs in the universe can be constructed from them:

1. Basic actions
2. Looping actions
3. Choice actions

Again, this notion is not shared by all programmers. Programming as a mystical form of science is a concept purposely maintained and promoted by many programmers in order to keep their jobs. Programming is intellectually tough, but adding mystery to an activity that is already too cryptic for many of its practitioners is inexcusable.

The Complex Program Myth. Programming is difficult because it is inherently complex to write instructions for a computer.

Fact. Programming is only as difficult as the problem being solved, and every problem solution can be broken down into combinations of the three simple actions (*basic, looping,* and *choice*).

The speedcode notation for these three intellectually manageable blocks is very straightforward. First, the *basic* actions are written as an assignment statement.

```
Y:= (X + 5) * (Z — S)
```

We can combine *basic* actions and the other two kinds of building blocks in various ways to form complete modules. Thus, several *basic* actions may be placed together with the *looping* action and *choice* action.

```
SUM:= 0;
    I:= 0
while (I < N) loop
    SUM:= SUM + ARRAY(I);
        I:= I + 1
end loop
```

The speedcode above computes the sum of array elements 0 through (N — 1). The *looping* action used to describe the summation calculation has a skeleton of the following form.

```
while (predicate) loop;
____
____
____
end loop;
```

The beginning of the loop is indicated by the keyword **loop,** and termination shown by **end loop.** The **while** clause contains a *predicate* that tells the computer when to skip the loop body and when to execute the loop body. Thus, as long as the predicate is *true,* the loop is repeated.

```
INOUT: procedure ( );
          var              I : byte
          var      LINE (10) : byte
          var             CH : byte
          const            N : byte = 11
          const           CR : byte = 13
          CH:= 0;
          I:= 0; while (I < N or CH not = CR) loop
                 CH:= INPUTK;
                 OUTPUTS (CH);
                 LINE(I):= CH;
                 I:= I = 1;
                 end loop
WRITE: loop;
                 CH:= LINE (N — I)
                 OUTPUTL (CH);
                 I:= I — 1;
                 end loop when (I = 0);
FINISH: OUTPUTK (12);
                 OUTPUTL (12);
                 return;
       end INOUT
```

Fig. 1.3 Speedcode as **BLUE₁** specification language.

Another form of the *looping* action is sometimes useful, especially when the predicate is to be tested at the end of the loop. This is the **loop until,** or **end loop when** form.

```
loop
end loop when (predicate);
```

This form of iteration is repeated until the predicate is *true*. The loop is repeated for every time the predicate is tested and found to be *false*. We could write the equivalent of the **while** loop in **when (until)** loop form as follows.

```
SUM:= 0;
   I:= 0; loop
       SUM:= SUM + ARRAY(I);
          I:= I + 1
       end loop when (I = N);
```

In this form, the loop will always be executed at least once, but in the **while** form the loop predicate may prevent any iteration at all. This difference may be of concern to a programmer trying to write reliable code.

The keyboard–input–printer–output program previously mentioned may be used again to illustrate the methods of speedcode. Figure 1.3 shows a complete speedcode specification of this problem. The OUT-PUTS routine is a module that outputs a character to the CRT screen. The OUTPUTL and OUTPUTK routines drive the line printer and keyboard, respectively. The refinement of speedcode to kludgecode for the Intel 8080 and Motorola 6800 microprocessors will be presented in the next few chapters.

The third building block will now be examined. It is the *choice action* construct.

```
if (predicate) then
          LABEL1: _____
                  _____
                  _____
                  _____
          else
          LABEL2: _____
                  _____
                  _____
end if
```

The construct begins with an **if** keyword and ends with the keyword **end if**. It is a compound block because at LABEL1 and LABEL2 we allow nested statements of any kind, including additional **if** statements.

The **if** statement allows the programmer to execute different sections of code depending on the values of certain variables. An example will help demonstrate the power of this block. Suppose we want to read a string of ASCII numerals from the keyboard of some microcomputer. The input may be alphanumic—it is possible that values other than the digits 0-9 are admitted. We can choose to ignore them in the following manner.

```
CH:= INPUTK
if (CH < "9"
   and CH > "0") then
              DO IT: _____
                     _____
                     _____
              else
              DON'T: _____
                     _____
                     _____
end if;
```

This segment of code causes the clause at label DO IT to be executed when the input character is a numeral; otherwise, the clause DON'T is executed.

Often the **else** clause is not needed in a speedcode specification. In such a case the clause is dropped.

```
if (predicate) then
          LABEL1: _____
                  _____
                  _____
                  _____

end if;
```

Notice that the speedcode building blocks define a subprocedure call as one of the *basic actions* rather than as a separate building block. This is intentional, because the subprocedures are *not essential* to writing programs. They are very helpful, but not required. Hence, from only three action blocks we are able to write any program.

Additional building blocks are introduced in the following chapters. They are mere conveniences and, like subprocedures, are not essential to programming. We introduce them to make programming easier, and in some cases more reliable.

Let's turn next to the central task of developing million dollar software for ten dollar microcomputers. Remember the lessons of this chapter:

1. Planning
2. Levels of abstraction—blueprints
3. Modularize—decompose programs
4. Limited control structures—speedcode
5. Consider testing early in the design

Also remember that every program can be implemented using the building blocks of speedcode:

a. Basic actions: **add, sub, move**
b. Looping actions: **while, until**
c. Choice actions: **if then else**

2
Plan Ahead

I once knew a race-car driver with the daring of a swashbuckler, the reflexes of a jaguar, and the trophies to prove it. He amazed spectators by doing the impossible.

I recall an interview with him: "How do you manage to squeeze through the other cars on those tight turns?" The announcer thrust a microphone into his face.

"I don't worry about that until I have to," said the smiling driver.

"Well, you must have some special technique, sir," the announcer probed.

"I wish I did," he whipped, "but I just get by, somehow."

The driver wasn't hiding a secret technique as it turned out. He lasted only one season.

*   *   *

Data Decomposition and Graffiti Charts

Professional programmers individually or collectively develop methods of decomposing large programs into a collection of small programs. The modularity of a program determines its difficulty to some degree, and this concept will be addressed here.

We illustrated modular decomposition very briefly in the previous chapter. The purpose of modular decomposition is to streamline the software system. Consequently, this part of the refinement process is called *streamlining*.

A software system is streamlined by decomposition of its data and modules. A data decomposition strategy develops a collection of modules by first diagramming the problem as a *graffiti chart*, shown in Fig. 2.1.

Figure 2.1 is a data decomposition analysis of the keyboard–input–printer–output program analyzed in Chapter 1. We see from this graffiti chart that the input data is a collection of *data chunks* called INSTRING and CHAR. In fact, the INSTRING entity is composed of a lot of CHAR entities, as indicated by the * above CHAR.

The output string OUTSTRING is composed of a number of ANYCHAR entities and a carriage return CR. In addition, the LF (line feed) character is output.

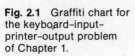

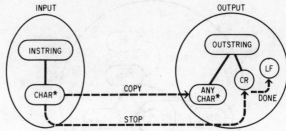

Fig. 2.1 Graffiti chart for the keyboard–input– printer–output problem of Chapter 1.

We have drawn dotted lines between the input entities and their corresponding output entities to show the transformation of inputs to outputs. Each dotted line is labeled with the name of a routine that transforms the input data into output data. Thus, the COPY routine causes the characters from INSTRING to be copied to the OUTSTRING. The STOP routine causes a CR to be output, and in turn causes the DONE routine to be executed.

The graffiti chart provides a different way of viewing a system of modules. It is a view from the *data* vantage point rather than the *module* vantage point. It is a powerful tool used to decompose large systems into smaller ones.

Suppose we design a system for a chemist that incorporates a data-acquisition program. The problem is to read single-byte data from a chemical experiment and "watch" the data until it begins to increase in value. We mark the beginning point as the START value, and continue to monitor the data. When the incoming values reach a maximum, we mark this point as the PEAK, and continue to monitor the inputs. Finally, the values decline until they again reach a minimum; we mark this as the STOP point.

Figure 2.2 is a data decomposition of the problem, while Fig. 2.3 is a graph of the chemist's PEAK data. Since the data is coming in at a very low rate (one point per second), the microprocessor has lots of time time left to do other things. Thus, the solution must take this into consideration.

A STATUS value is kept by the microprocessor. Whenever the next data byte is waiting to be input to the processing program, the STATUS value is set to READY to alert the processor of the availability of data. This is called *interrupt driven* programming.

In an interrupt driven program, we set up a procedure to handle the interrupt in exactly the same way we introduce a subroutine into a computer. The difference is that the microprocessor calls the subroutine when the STATUS is READY, rather than through execution of a JSR instruction.

The manner in which microcomputers call interrupt subprograms is not the main concern here, and this mechanism will be discussed later.

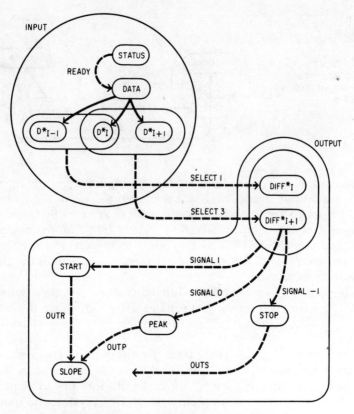

Fig. 2.2 Graffiti chart for chemist's application.

For now we need only treat the solution as if it were an ordinary sub-routine. Each time the subroutine is *called* it transfers a single byte into the computer's memory, processes it, and then returns to the program that was interrupted (this other program is doing extensive processing on some other function).

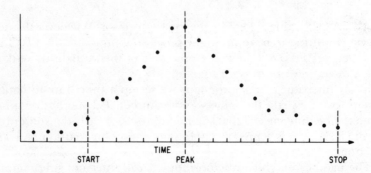

Fig. 2.3 An example of the chemist's data.

The data decomposition of Fig. 2.2 begins by inputting a status value into STATUS. This in turn causes READY to invoke the subroutine we are trying to design. The subroutine reads data, beginning with D_{I-1} and subsequently D_I, and finally D_{I+1}. When two values are obtained, they are differenced in order to compute the slope of the graph (see Fig. 2.3).

The SELECT1 operator computes the first difference, $DIFF_I$. The SELECT3 operator computes the subsequent difference, $DIFF_{I+1}$. The chemist defined the problem to his programmer in the following blueprint form.

BLUE$_0$

1. Wait for each data byte.
2. When it comes, use it to compute a difference, or SLOPE.
3. Whenever two consecutive SLOPEs are above or below a THRESHOLD value (a number set by the chemist), we change the SLOPE to indicate a START, STOP, or PEAK value.
4. Use the following logic:

```
START
      when SLOPE = 0 and DIFF₁ > THRESHOLD
                      and DIFF₁₊₁ > THRESHOLD
      change SLOPE to +1.
PEAK
      When SLOPE = 1 and DIFF₁ < —THRESHOLD
                      and DIFF₁₊₁ < —THRESHOLD
      change SLOPE to —1.
STOP
      When SLOPE = —1 and —THRESHOLD < DIFF₁ < THRESHOLD
                       and —THRESHOLD < DIFF₁₊₁ < THRESHOLD
      change SLOPE to 0.
```

5. Output the value of I for each START, STOP, and PEAK value located in this manner.
6. Ignore all other data values.

end BLUE$_0$

The chemist's problem is ready to be modularized and written in speedcode. Let's continue to use it as an example in the next section on modular decomposition.

Module Decomposition with the Dynamic Trio

Before we continue with the modular decomposition of the chemist's problem we introduce a new structure that is more convenient than nested **if** blocks. Suppose we want to select one of many paths through a program. The example below uses *nested if* clauses to select one of three paths through the program, depending on the value of variable FLAG.

```
var FLAG : byte
            _____
            _____
            _____
        if (FLAG = 0) then
                   ZERO: _____
                         _____
                         _____
                 else
                 NONZ: if (FLAG = 1) then
                               one: _____
                                    _____
                                    _____
                       else
                       NON1: if (FLAG = 2) then
                                     TWO: _____
                                          _____
                                          _____
                             end if;
                   end if;
        end if;
```

This is much too complicated for the simple task we demand of the program. Thus, we introduce a more convenient, but nonessential building block called *select case*. It does the same thing, but in a simpler fashion.

```
case FLAG of
     "0": _____
          _____
          _____
     "1": _____
          _____
          _____
     "2": _____
          _____
          _____
end case
```

The case is terminated by **end case.** Note that the segments contained within each choice will run into the following segments of code unless we prevent this from happening. Thus we use an **exitcase** keyword to break out of the **case** block.

```
case FLAG of; .
     "0": _____
          _____
          _____
          exitcase;
     "1": _____
          _____
          _____
          exitcase;
```

```
        "2": _____
              _____
              _____
              exitcase;
    end case;
```

Now lets return to the chemist's problem and develop the modules needed to solve the interrupt driven problem. We use module decomposition to construct the **BLUE₁** specification in speedcode. The following is a first-order approximation to the final solution.

```
    BLUE₁
        PEAK: interrupt procedure ( );
                var FLAG         : byte = 0
                var DIFFI        : byte
                var DIFFI1       : byte
                var DI           : byte
                var SLOPE        : byte = 0
                var START        : byte
                var PEAK         : byte
                var STOP         : byte
                var I            : byte
                const THRESH : byte = 25
                I:= I + 1;
        SELECT: case FLAG of;
                        "0": DI:= INPUT;
                             FLAG:= 1;
                             return;
                        "1": DIFFI:= INPUT — DI
                             FLAG:= 2;
                             return;
                        "2": DI:= INPUT;
                             FLAG:= 3;
                             return;
                        "3": DIFFI:= INPUT — DI;
                             FLAG:= 0;
        SIGNAL: case SLOPE of;
                        "—1": if (DIFFI < THRESH
                             and DIFFI < THRESH
                             and DIFFI > —THRESH
                             and DIFFI1 > —THRESH)
                                  then
                                  OUTS: SLOPE:= 0
                                        STOP (I);
                             end if;
                             return;
                        "0": if (DIFFI > THRESH
                             and DIFFI1 > THRESH)
                             then
                             OUTR: SLOPE:= 1;
                                   START (I)
                             end if;
                             return;
                        "1": if (DIFFI < —THRESH
                             and DIFFI1 < —THRESH)
```

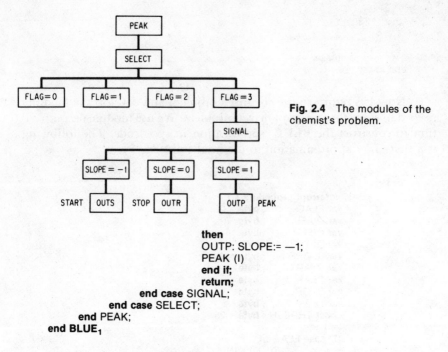

Fig. 2.4 The modules of the chemist's problem.

```
              then
              OUTP: SLOPE:= —1;
              PEAK (I)
              end if;
              return;
        end case SIGNAL;
     end case SELECT;
  end PEAK;
end BLUE₁
```

The chemist's program counts the number of data points input to it and stores this value in variable I. When FLAG = 0, the first value needed in computing DIFFI is stored in DI. The value of FLAG is changed to one so the next time the routine is called we will compute the difference (FLAG = 1).

By the time we work up to FLAG = 3, the two differences are computed and ready to be compared with the THRESHOLD value stored in THRESH.

Note how the values are selected in groups of four. After the first four values are used to compute the two differences, the process begins again with four new values. In order to alter this approach to one using a sliding difference, we would have to save the input values as they are read in. The program would be more complex, but the idea remains the same.

A modular decomposition of the chemist's problem is shown in Fig. 2.4. At the top of the hierarchy we define the procedure PEAK. Using the data decomposition modules we streamline the SELECT module into a separate case (FLAG = 7) for each value of FLAG. The last value for FLAG (FLAG = 3) results in additional streamlining.

The code for SIGNAL is a streamlined case construct for each value of SLOPE. These in turn, call one of the routines, OUTR, OUTS, or OUTP. The output routines cause the appropriate value of START, STOP, or PEAK locations to be printed.

We will learn how to streamline the $BLUE_1$ program level even further in the next two chapters. Before doing so, however, a few words of caution.

Keep It Simple, Speedcoder

Simplicity is the central goal of the Electrifying, Streamlined Blueprint Speedcode Method. We managed to maintain simplicity in the chemist's problem by introducing the **case** building block. In the following programming examples, we will constantly battle complexity. In particular, when we transform the $BLUE_1$ code into a particular microprocessor assembly language, the temptation to complicate the result will loom up as a difficult problem.

We can cope with complexity in several ways. They are broadly classified as follows.

1. Information hiding
2. Psychological chunking
3. Reduce connectivity

Levels of abstraction can be used to hide details that are not useful in the beginning of software refinement (streamlining). At successive levels of refinement, we introduce details in chunks. This is easy to do only after the bigger chunks are well understood. Information hiding allows us to concentrate on only a small part of the problem at a time.

Psychological chunking is used by everyone to solve problems. It is a known fact that the human mind is capable of retaining no more than about seven facts simultaneously. Thus, we must streamline blueprints into modules of no more than seven submodules, and break submodules into no more than seven sub-submodules, etc.

In practical terms, four to five nested loops border on the unreliable for our purposes. We also should avoid nesting **if** clauses inside one another beyond four to five levels.

Finally, complexity can manifest itself in terms of the connectivity of modules. We say a module is *K-ways connected* to another module if there are K variables shared by, passed to, or passed-back from one module to the other.

A module may be too small if K-way connectivity is large. Likewise, a module is too large if K is very small. The exact numerical value of K is not known to software engineers, but for our purposes the value of K will lie between one and seven.

In short, the disciple of the speedcode method must constantly be on guard for creeping complexity. *Remember: The program for a problem solution should be only as complex as the problem itself.*

3
Never Write
a Large Program

Three programmers left home to find their fortunes in computer country. The first programmer built his fortune on 150,000 lines of assembly language code. One day the rains of business venture came and washed away the machine used by the first programmer. It also washed away the 150,000 lines of machine-dependent code.

The second programmer invested his fortune-seeking efforts in 30,000 lines of Fortran code. One day his supervisor came along and huffed and puffed until he blew the Fortran listings into the trash can. The supervisor told him to learn a microprocessor assembly language because their new microprocessor had no Fortran compiler.

The third programmer never wrote large programs. Instead, he collected about 100 speedcode modules that incorporated all the basic algorithms he learned while working as a programmer. So far, he has refined the speedcode modules onto eight different computers in three different languages. One day his supervisor huffed and puffed until he blew away the programs. The next day, the third programmer took a job with the competitor company at twice his previous salary. He took his speedcode modules with him.

* * *

The Stacked Computer

The largest programs in the world can be broken into small pieces. This is done by modularizing and applying the building block method to the modules. We have discussed alternate methods of decomposing programs in the previous chapter. The point illustrated in this chapter is the idea that *programmers don't have to write large programs unless they purposely choose to.*

Indeed, the error rate of programs is directly related to the size of the program. Furthermore, the programming effort for developing a program of size S increases exponentially as S increases:

$$\text{Effort} = CS^{1.5}$$

22

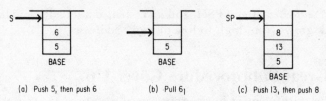

(a) Push 5, then push 6   (b) Pull 6₁   (c) Push 13, then push 8

Fig. 3.1   Operation of a stack.

where C is the application constant and S is the number of statements in a program. Hence, we are punished in two ways whenever large programs are attempted: The effort zooms, and the probability that programs won't work properly increases.

The solution to this problem is simple: *never write a large program.* How can we do this? *By refining small program segments into assembly language code in a step-by-step fashion.* The process is called streamlining the blueprints. But first we need some tools.

A *pushdown stack,* or simply *stack,* is a data structure for storing data in a computer memory. The last datum placed in the stack memory is the first datum to be removed. The stack is a last-in, first-out storage mechanism. Figure 3.1 illustrates the operation of a stack.

The base of a stack is the address in main memory of the first available storage byte in the stack. The top of the stack is the address of the stack storage element next in line to be "pushed" or "pulled." A stack pointer SP is usually associated with the top of stack (TOS) element. We call each storage space in the stack a *frame.* Thus, the TOS frame is the location of the last datum pushed onto the stack, and the next datum to be pulled.

In Fig. 3.1, the SP points to the next available frame after 5 and 6 have been pushed onto the stack. If we pull (or pop) the stack, we copy the value on the TOS into some other memory location and cause the SP to *move up the stack.*

Most microprocessors have stack operations for loading the SP with a base address, and for push and pull operations on the stack. For example, the Motorola 6800 provides for stack operation as follows.

```
LDS        #BASE      **set up BASE
LDA A      #5
PSH A                 **push 5
LDA A      #6
PSH A                 **push 6
PUL A                 **copy 6 into A
```

The LDS (load stack) operation initializes the SP register by loading the address of BASE into SP. The PSH and PUL operations cause the data to be copied from accumulator A to the TOS and vice versa. The SP register is *decremented* after a PSH, and *incremented* after a PUL. This means the stack grows from high to low memory addresses.

The Great Subprocedure Cover-Up

The stack of most microprocessors is also used to store the return addresses generated by a subroutine call. For example, when executing a JSR (jump subroutine) instruction, the current value of PC (program counter) is replaced with the starting address of the subroutine. The previous value of PC is saved on the stack by pushing the upper and lower 8-bit bytes onto the two TOS frames.

The return operation RTS (return from subroutine) will remove the two bytes from the TOS frames and restore these to the PC. This produces a return to the instruction following the *call*.

```
          ─────
          JSR   SUBR
NEXT      LDA A
          ─────

          ─────
SUBR      NOP
```

The value of NEXT is pushed onto the stack when JSR is executed. The value of SUBR is placed in the PC register. When the RTS instruction is executed, the value of NEXT is pulled from the TOS frames and placed in the PC. Thus, the main program continues from its previous place.

Often, the JSR will cause the return address to be placed on the stack when we do not desire it to happen. For example, if values are placed on the TOS as parameters to a subroutine, then the subroutine will have to remove the two TOS (return address) frames and save them until the return is executed. This can be done in Motorola 6800 assembler code as follows.

```
SUBROUT   PUL   A
          STA   A    SAVE
          PUL   A
          STA   A    SAVE + 1

          ─────
          ─────
          LDA   A    SAVE + 1
          PSH   A
          LDA   A    SAVE
          PSH   A
          RTS
SAVE      RMB        2
          END
```

The stack is used to hold the return address of a subprocedure because the return sequence for a consecutive sequence of subprocedure calls is last-in, first-out. Thus, the order of returning from nested calls is also the order imposed by the stack. This notion is illustrated by the nested calls, below.

```
JSR    S1
____
____
____
S1         ____
           ____
           JSR    S2
           ____
           ____
           RTS
       S2  ____
           ____
           JSR    S3
           ____
           ____
           RTS
       S3      ____
               ____
               ____
               RTS
```

Suppose the main program calls subprocedure S1, which calls subroutine S2, which calls S3. The return addresses must be stacked in order for the returns to retrace their path, backwards; S3 to S2, S2 to S1.

The pushdown stack is useful for storage of intermediate results and return addresses. We have shown how both are accomplished in a microprocessor. Next, we develop a streamlining method for refining speedcode into kludgecode using the stack manipulation capability found in most microprocessors.

Basic Actions Are Easy, Bucky

The *basic* actions of a microprocessor are loads, stores, addition, subtraction, comparisons, push, pull, etc. They are simple instructions available in the instruction sets of all computers at some level.

The kludgecode manifestations of these basic actions vary from microprocessor to microprocessor, but the concepts remain the same. On some micros, the kludgecode must be "bent" to conform to the programmer's will, while on other microprocessors the streamlined code is straightforward.

The Motorola 6800 kludgecode offers the most straightforward approach to streamlining the speedcode specifications of a program. It is

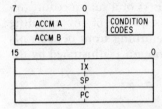

Fig. 3.2　The Motorola 6800 architecture.

```
a. Load and store kludgecode
     LDA  A    LABEL    load register A
     STA  A    LABEL    store register A
     LDA  B    LABEL    load register B
     STA  B    LABEL    store register B
     LDS       LABEL    load stack pointer (SP)
     STS       LABEL    store stack pointer (SP)
     LDX       LABEL    load index register (IX)
     STX       LABEL    store index register (IX)

b. Stack operation kludgecode
     PSH  A             push register A onto the stack
     PSH  B             push register B onto the stack
     PUL  A             pull TOS into register A
     PUL  B             pull TOS into register B

c. Arithmetic
     ADD  A    LABEL    add contents of LABEL to A
     SUB  A    LABEL    subtract from A
     ADD  B    LABEL    add contents of LABEL to B
     SUB  B    LABEL    subtract from B
```

a simple processor with simple instructions (see Fig. 3.2), containing a few of the most commonly used kludgecode mnemonics.

The Intel 8080 kludgecode offers the programmer a greater variety of kludgecode mnemonics to employ, most of which will not be used here because they are not essential. Indeed, in some cases the 8080 kludgecode is harmful because it leads to incorrect implementations. The sampling of 8080 kludgecode in Fig. 3.3 represents the majority of mnemonics used in this chapter when dealing with the 8080.

When using either microprocessor, the particular instructions needed and used in streamlining will exceed those shown in the lists of Figs. 3.2 and 3.3. When in doubt about the operation of the microprocessor, the reader should consult the programmer's reference manual or user's guide for the particular microprocessor being used. The streamlining process works equally well with any microprocessor, but we will use only the 6800 and 8080 in our examples.

The first demonstration of streamlining *basic* actions considers a simple assignment statement.

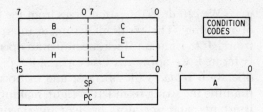

Fig. 3.3 The Intel 8080 architecture.

a. Load and store kludgecode

LDA	LABEL	load A directly from LABEL
STA	LABEL	store A directly to LABEL
MOV	toreg,fromreg	copy from register, to register
MVI	toreg,constant	load a constant into a register
LXI	SP,constant	initialize the stack pointer
LHLD	LABEL	load the HL register pair

b. Stack operations (always takes 2 bytes)

PUSH	PSW	pushes A and the condition codes
PUSH	reg pair	pushes register pairs; BC, DE, or HL
POP	reg pair	pulls register pairs; BC, DE, or HL

c. Arithmetic

ADD	register	add "register" to A
ADI	constant	add a "constant" to A
SUB	register	subtract "register" from A
SUI	constant	subtract a "constant" from A

```
var        S : byte
var        T : byte
var        Y : byte
const   FIVE : byte
Y:= (S + FIVE) — (T + Y);
```

This segment of code can be streamlined into 6800 kludgecode by first using RMB2 (reserve memory bytes) for the declarations. Then the expression for Y is rewritten in *postfix notation*. Finally, kludgecode is generated from the postfix notation in a very rigid, consistent (reliable), manner.

To get the expression into postfix notation:

1. Every variable and constant is written in order, from left to right, as it appears in the expression. Thus, for the demonstration above we have

$$Y \quad S \quad FIVE \quad T \quad Y$$

2. Every operator is placed *immediately following* the variables and constants obtained from the first rule. Parenthesized subexpressions and intermediate results are considered variables when placing the operators in the postfix notation. Hence, we complete the example, above:

$$(Y \quad ((S \quad FIVE \quad +) \quad (T \quad Y \quad +) \quad - \quad) \quad := \quad)$$

We can drop the parentheses from the postfix notation without loss of meaning. The resultant string is interpreted very simply: We read from left to right until we encounter an operator. When the first operator is located, we apply it to the operand(s) preceding it. The *result* of the operation *replaces* the operator and its operand(s). We then continue to examine the string from left to right, making sure to replace the variables, constants, and operators by their intermediate results. The step-by-step reduction of the sample above yields the correct result for evaluating the speedcode expression.

```
Y      S      FIVE     +      T      Y      +      —      :=
                     do this

Y      (S + FIVE)             T      Y      +      —      :=
                                          do this

Y      (S + FIVE)                    (T + Y)           —      :=
                                                    do this

Y      ((S + FIVE) — (T + Y))                                :=
                                                           do this

(Y:= ((S + FIVE) — (T + Y)))
```

How can we use this method to get the kludgecode equivalent? We use the stack to examine the postfix notation from left to right. When an operation is located the variables and constants are pulled from the stack, the indicated operations are performed, and the result is stored on the stack. Note that the first variable is skipped. This is because it is being used to store the result (:=).

Y	S	FIVE	+	T	Y	+	—	:=
skip	push	push	pull	push	push	pull	pull	pull
Y	Y	FIVE	ADD	T	Y	ADD	SUB	STORE

We are now in a position to develop kludgecode for this expression. The first version will be in 6800 kludgecode, the second in 8080 kludgecode. Note the differences and similarities.

BLUE$_2$: 6800 kludgecode for Y:= (S + FIVE) — (T + Y)
```
*   skip Y
*
    LDA A S
    PSH A                    **push S
    LDA A FIVE
    PSH A                    **push FIVE
*   pull and add
    PUL A                    **get FIVE
    PUL B                    **get S
    ABA                      **(S + FIVE)
    PSH A                    **push (S + FIVE)
*   continue left to right
```

```
        LDA A T
        PSH A
        LDA A Y
        PSH A              **push Y
*   pull and add
        PUL A              **get Y
        PUL B              **get T
        ABA                **(T + Y)
        PSH A              **push (T + Y)
*   pull and subtract
        PUL B              **get (T + Y)
        PUL A              **get (S + FIVE)
        SBA                **(S + FIVE) — (T + Y)
        PSH A              **push (S + FIVE) — (T + Y)
*   pull and store
        PUL A              **get (S + FIVE) — (T + Y)
        STA A Y            **Y:=
end BLUE₂
```

Clearly, this code is correct, though inefficient. Recall the rule concerning modularity. The corollary of this rule is "Make it correct, *then* make it fast." We have used this corollary to produce correct code, assuming overflows do not occur during addition and subtraction. Additional shorthand techniques will be examined in Chapter Five. Now, we are concerned only with demonstrating how to streamline programs to obtain kludgecode. You may choose to eliminate redundant PSH and PUL instructions from the kludgecode given above. Here we continue to use the same calculation, this time implemented in the Intel 8080 language.

```
BLUE₂: 8080 kludgecode
;   skip       Y
;
;
        LDA        S
        PUSH       PSW    ;  **push S and condition codes
        LDA        FIVE
        PUSH       PSW    ;  **push FIVE and condition codes
;   pull and add
        POP        PSW    ;  **get FIVE
        MOV        B, A   ;  **save in B
        POP        PSW    ;  **get S
        ADD        B      ;  **(S + FIVE)
        PUSH       PSW    ;  **push (S + FIVE)
;   continue left to right
        LDA        T
        PUSH       PSW    ;  **push T
        LDA        Y      ;
        PUSH       PSW    ;  **push Y
;   pull and add
        POP        PSW    ;
        MOV        B, A   ;  **get Y
        POP        PSW    ;  **get T
        ADD        B      ;  **(T + Y)
        PUSH       PSW    ;  **push (T + Y)
;   pull and subtract
        POP        PSW
```

```
        MOV      B, A        ;  **get (T + Y)
        POP      PSW         ;  **get (S + FIVE)
        SUB      B           ;  **(S + FIVE) — (T + Y)
        PUSH     PSW         ;  **(S + FIVE) — (T + Y)
;  pull and store
        POP      PSW         ;  **get (S ⸱ FIVE) — (T + Y)
        STA      Y           ;  **Y:=
end BLUE₂
```

As can be seen by comparison of the two versions, the 8080 always pushes and pops two registers at a time. Furthermore, the MOV command is used to load register B whenever we want to remove the stack frame and place it in register B. This is done by POPing PSW, then MOVing from A to B.

The generality of the streamline method can be illustrated with a more complex example. Suppose we attempt a computation that is beyond the power of the *basic* actions.

```
var      S : byte
var      T : byte
var      Y : byte
const FIVE : byte = 5
        Y:= S * T + FIVE
```

In the expression for Y we perform a multiply operation that is usually not part of the basic capability of most microprocessors. How is this handled?

The postfix notation for this calculation is straightforward.

$$Y \quad S \quad T \quad * \quad FIVE \quad + \quad :=$$

But what kludgecode is generated when the * is encountered? Here is an opportunity to use the stack and the subroutine capabilities of most microprocessors.

```
BLUE₂: 6800
*   skip Y
*
        LDA   A       S
        PSH   A                   **push S
        LDA   T
        PSH   A                   **push T
*   use a subroutine to calculate the product
        JSR           MULT1   **(S * T)
*   product is put on the TOS
        LDA   A       FIVE
        PSH   A                   **push FIVE
*   now add
        PUL   B                   **get FIVE into B
        PUL   A                   **get (S * T)
        ABA                       **(S * T) + 5
        PSH   A                   **push result
```

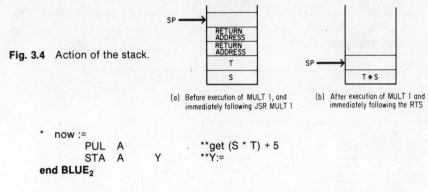

Fig. 3.4 Action of the stack.

(a) Before execution of MULT 1, and
immediately following JSR MULT 1

(b) After execution of MULT 1 and
immediately following the RTS

```
*   now :=
          PUL   A              **get (S * T) + 5
          STA   A        Y     **Y:=
   end BLUE₂
```

The JSR code in this version will cause the subprocedure MULT1 to be executed. But we must be careful about using the stack for return addresses and for passing numbers to a subprocedure. In Fig. 3.4 we show the status of the pushdown stack at the beginning of routine MULT1, and again when the return has been accomplished.

In order to "simulate" the multiply operation, we need more than the *basic* actions. Therefore we will postpone the development of routine MULT1 until the next chapter. Note, however, that the MULT1 subprocedure must remove the "return address" frames from the top of stack in order to access the values passed to it. Furthermore, the routine must replace them on the TOS before an RTS (return subroutine in the 6800) or a RET (return subroutine in the 8080) is executed.

The JSR and CALL kludgecodes are *basic* actions that extend the power of a microprocessor system. They allow more complex operations to be "simulated" by collections of *basic* actions and the control actions discussed in the next chapter.

Other *basic* actions helpful to the microprocessor programmer include shift operations, rotation, and comparisons. A short example of the latter will demonstrate the concept and prepare us for the next chapter.

Suppose we want to evaluate the truth of the expression:

$$I < (Y + S/2) \, ?$$

If I is "less than" as suggested above, then the expression is *true*, otherwise the expression is *false*. An expression that can be either *true* or *false* is called a *Boolean expression*, or a *predicate*. Predicates are evaluated in computers in much the same fashion as numeric expressions. The following blueprint kludgecode illustrates this.

Let the postfix notation guide the production of kludgecode.

$$I \quad Y \quad S \quad 2 \quad / \quad + \quad <$$

We skip over I, initially, then push the variables Y, S, and 2, onto the TOS. When the / is reached we call a subroutine to do division. The DIV1 routine produces two results: the integer remainder and quotient. The remainder is deleted from the blueprint, while the quotient is used to evaluate the predicate.

```
BLUE₂: 6800
*   I  Y  S  2  /  +  <
*   skip I
*
        .  LDA   A        Y     **push Y
           PSH   A              **onto TOS
           LDA   A        S
           PSH   A              **stack S
           LDA   A        #2    **immediate addressing
           PSH   A              **stack 2
           JSR            DIV1  **simulate divide
           PUL   A              **discard remainder
           PUL   A              **get (S/2)
           PUL   B              **get Y
           ABA                  **Y + (S/2)
*   instead of :=, compare
           LDA   B        I     **get I
           CBA                  **compare: A–B?
*   set the condition code here
end BLUE₂
```

The result of executing the kludgecode for < is to set the appropriate condition codes on the microprocessor. In the next instruction, the condition code may be tested and a branch executed, depending on the value of the condition code.

A similar result is obtained in the 8080 architecture using (lavishly) the two-byte PUSH and POP equivalents to the 6800 PSH and PUL instructions.

```
BLUE₂: 8080
;   I  Y  S  2  /  +  <
;   skip I
;
        LDA   Y
        PUSH  PSW        ;   **push Y
        LDA   S
        PUSH  PSW        ;   **push S
        MVI   A, 02H     ;   **get constant
        PUSH  PSW
        CALL  DIV1       ;   **simulate divide
        POP   PSW        ;   **discard remainder
        POP   PSW        ;   **get quotient (S/2)
        MOV   B, A       ;   **put (S/2) in B
        POP   PSW        ;   **get Y back
        ADD   B          ;   **Y + (S/2)
;   instead of :=, compare
        MOV   B, A       ;   **short-out to B
        LDA   I          ;   **get I
        CMP   B          ;   **compare: A–B?
;   set the condition code here
end BLUE₂
```

The condition code setting is used to branch forward or backward in kludgecode. However, branching is, in general, very risky in programming. Therefore, we need several more carefully chosen mechanisms for branching in microprocessor programs. In the next chapter we develop the final mechanisms promised earlier. With these, we can write any program.

4
Program in Levels of Abstraction

Mike was a slow, methodical programmer. Some people even considered him a hacker of less-than-average quality. Mike took two months longer to finish his last programming project than his supervisor wanted him to. In fact, the microprocessor memory containing Mike's programs had to be increased by 20% to hold all of the code he produced. The company finally had to invest an additional $800,000 to cover the added cost. But it worked, and the product made money for the company.

* * *

Joe was a fast thinker, fast talker, and fast coder. Joe finished the programs of his last project before anyone else on the team and, in fact, saved the company money by allowing a decrease of the memory size required to hold the programs. The project was a commercial success, and the company would have been well on its way to a profit, except for one thing. Joe's team spent all of its time making small changes to the delivered systems. They spent thousands of dollars traveling to the customers in order to fix bugs, add features, and in general maintain the new system. After five years, the company withdrew the product and wrote it off as a loss because they could not afford to support it any longer.

* * *

Software engineers develop programs in parts. Each part can be better comprehended by use of abstractions—this simplifies programming. Such abstraction is the underlying concept of the streamlined blueprint method. In fact, software is most reliably developed using levels of abstraction.

An abstraction is a representation of an algorithm in some form that hides a certain amount of detail from view. The greater the amount of hidden detail, the more abstract is the program. Thus, a software blueprint represents algorithms at a level that ignores implementation details. A computer program in speedcode form also represents the algorithms of a software system, but shows greater detail. Finally, more detail is introduced by kludgecode. Each form of the algorithm is a level of abstraction.

We will be concerned with the following levels of abstraction:

overview blueprints
psuedocode blueprints
speedcode blueprints
kludgecode
machine code

We also refine each of these levels by divide-and-conquer techniques:

modularity
subroutines
code sections

These techniques are used at various levels of abstraction to help us comprehend the software implementation. It is a form of psychological chunking used to lower the number of details one must recall while programming.

In this chapter we use subroutining to cover-up the microprocessor architecture. An architecture is covered by subroutining whenever we replace an undesirable architectural feature with a subroutine that simulates a desirable feature. The most obvious example is in the area of data structures.

In the next few sections we cover-up the tedious flag and weak array subscripting features of microprocessors by simulation subroutines. These subroutines raise the level of abstraction, thereby removing some of the detail that would constantly get in the way of implementors. Fortunately, the detail needs to be dealt with only once, and then concealed by an appropriate subroutine.

Computers Have Indecision

The stack and *basic* actions give programmers enough power to perform most routine calculations. The major advantage of a microprocessor-controlled system is in the decision-making ability of such an intelligent controller. In order to make decisions, the microprocessor must include (a) condition codes for indicating side conditions after every instruction is executed, and (b) instructions to manipulate and test the condition codes.

The Intel 8080 and Motorola 6800 microprocessors, for example, incorporate a *flag register* containing single-bit condition code indicators.

Z: zero result
C: carry bit
N: negative (sometimes called P)
O: overflow (sometimes called V)
H: half-carry (sometimes called X)

The half-carry bit indicates the result of a carry-out from bit three (position four) of an 8-bit operation. This is used to adjust a binary operation to a BCD (binary-coded-decimal) operation. Thus, after an ADD, we could issue a decimal adjust DAA and produce a BCD result.

```
ADD        DATA10
DAA
STA        DATA10
```

This sequence of instructions takes two BCD encoded bytes, adds them (one is in register A), and stores the result as a byte at location DATA10. The H bit is used to accomplish this. (The H bit is often denoted with an X in the 8080.)

The remaining condition codes are used in obvious ways; the result of an arithmetic or logical operation sets the corresponding codes to indicate an overflow, carry, zero result, negative result, etc. These conditions are tested and often cause a program to execute in a different sequence, depending on the result of the test.

In the 8080 and 6800 microprocessor kludgecodes, we will use only a small subset of the possible decision instructions. The table below shows the most useful kludgecode mnemonics for each machine.

Intel 8080		Motorola 6800	Function
CMP	B	CBA	compare
CPI	immediate	CMP # immediate	
JZ	label	BEQ label	jump
JMP	label	BRA label	and
		JMP label	branch
JNZ	label	BNE label	not equal
JM	label	BLT label	less than
JP	label	BGT label	greater than
JZ	label⎫		
JM	label⎬	BLE label	less, and equal
JZ	label⎫		
JP	label⎬	BGE label	greater, and equal

Note in the table the rough correspondence between kludgecodes. In 6800 kludgecode a single instruction is capable of testing two condition code flags—it is BLE. In 8080 code we require two instructions to do the same thing.

The speedcode version of a condition code setting may require special designation. If we want to include a *carry* bit in an addition operation, for example, the **carry** and **nocarry** keywords may be employed. This idea is illustrated by the 16-bit addition routine below. Assuming the two, two-byte operants are passed to the ADDZ routine via the stack, we can specify a double-precision addition that returns a two-byte result to the stack.

```
BLUE₁: Speedcode for double add
ADD2: procedure  (TL: TOS byte,
                   TU: TOS byte,
                   SL: TOS byte,
                   SU: TOS byte)
      var TLOW : byte;
      var TUP  : byte;
      var SLOW : byte;
      var SUP  : byte;
      ;
      TLOW:= TL;
      TUP:= TU;
      SLOW:= SL + TLOW : nocarry;
      SUP:= SU + TUP   : carry;
      ;
      return (SLOW, SUP);
  end ADD2
  end BLUE₁
```

The streamlining of this speedcode produces a routine that must (a) save the return address, (b) do the appropriate addition with and without carry, and (c) restore the return address to the TOS position. The 6800 kludgecode below demonstrates what is involved. The reader should be able to generate an equivalent 8080 kludgecode listing by substitution from the previously mentioned table.

```
BLUE₂: Kludgecode for double add
*              procedure
     TLOW      RMB    1
     TUP       RMB    1
     SLOW      RMB    1
     SUP       RMB    1
     *
     ADD2      PUL    A
               STA    A  SAVE
               PUL    A
               STA    A  SAVE + 1      **save return address
     *  TLOW:= TL
               PUL    A
               STA    A  TLOW
     *  TUP:= TU
               PUL    A
               STA    A  TUP
     *  SLOW:= SL + TLOW : NOCARRY
               PUL    B                **get SL into ACCB
```

```
              LDA     A  TLOW
              CLC                        **clear carry flag: NOCARRY
              ABA                        **SL + TLOW
              STA     A  SLOW            **SLOW:= SL + TLOW
     *  SUP:= SU + TUP : CARRY
              PUL     A                  **get SU into ACCA
              LDA     B  TUP             **get TUP into ACCB
              ABC                        **SU + TUP: CARRY
              STA     A  SUP             **SUP:=
     *  push return result on TOS
              LDA     A  SUP
              PSH     A
              LDA     A  SLOW
              PSH     A                  **return values on TOS
     *  restore return address on TOS
              LDA     A  SAVE + 1
              PSH     A
              LDA     A  SAVE
              PSH     A
              RTS                        **return (SLOW, SUP)
  SAVE        RMB        2
              END
```

end BLUE$_2$

This version of ADD2 uses the 6800 kludgecode for placing a zero in the C flag; CLC. Other instructions are available in both the 6800 and 8080 microprocessors for setting these flags. It is also useful to note that many instructions do not affect the condition code values. For example, LDA and STA do not alter the condition code settings in either microprocessor. Be sure to investigate the possibility that the codes are altered when this is not desired. This can lead to an error in program execution.

The ADD2 routine can be put to immediate use if double-precision operations are needed. For example, the code below corresponds to a previously mentioned example. The ADD2 and MULT2 routines are used, though not shown.

```
var R : word
var S : word
var T : word
var Y : word
;
Y:= R * (S + T);
```

This speedcode defines 16-bit WORDs instead of 8-bit BYTEs. Thus, we will perform * and + in double-precision kludgecode. The corresponding 6800 kludgecode is given below.

```
  *    variables and storage
  R  RMB       2
  S  RMB       2
  T  RMB       2
  Y  RMB       2
```

```
*     Y:= R * (S + T);
      LDA   A      R              **upper half of R
      PSH   A
      LDA   A      R + 1          **lower half of R
      PSH   A
*
      LDA   A      S              **upper half of S
      PSH   A
      LDA   A      S + 1          **lower half of S
      PSH   A
*
      LDA   A      T              **upper half of T
      PSH   A
      LDA   A      T + 1          **lower half of T
      PSH   A
*     perform (S + T) in double precision
      JSR          ADD2           **(S + T) on TOS
*     perform R * (. . .)
      JSR          MULT2          **R * (S + T) on TOS
      PUL   A
      STA   A      Y + 1          **lower half
      PUL   A
      STA   A      Y
*     result is placed into Y and Y + 1 locations
```

This final example illustrates how easily we can adapt the Electrifying, Streamlined Blueprint Speedcode Method to multiple-precision calculations. The only modification involves adding code for the added data storage. This causes the program to be larger, but the methodology remains the same.

We next turn to the topic of decision making and how to use the branching and jump instructions reliably. These final instructions will allow us to write any and all computer programs in a reliable, efficient fashion.

To GOTO, or Not to GOTO, That Is the Question

The problem with branching and jump instructions is that they are responsible for a large percentage of errors in programs. It has been estimated that about 15% of all instructions used in large programs are branch instructions. Furthermore, these instructions account for more than 15% of the program patches resulting from debugging. If this is indeed true, then these instructions are more error-prone than they should be.

It has also been suggested that the free use of branching is the cause of its unreliable behavior. In a sense, the problem is that the branch instruction is too powerful. A programmer may abuse the power of a free branch, and in turn cause errors which are difficult to uncover.

If we restrict the use of branching to a smaller subset of possibilities, then we can hope to gain reliability, and in the bargain, gain an advantage for the programmer. How can we restrict the branch instruction without making it useless?

A very simple discipline will be employed *most of the time* when using branching statements.

> *The GOTO Rule.* Almost never use a GOTO. Only use it when code readability is *improved,* otherwise the branching statements are used to build *single-entry, single-exit* (SESE) control blocks in every program.

The notion of SESE blocks is very central to the structured programming methodology. It means that every program is composed of blocks with only one entry point, and only one exit point within the program. This restriction is not as great as it may seem at first glance. A few examples will illustrate the power of SESE structures.

We need only two additional control blocks to complete the list of essential programming tools. The *looping* actions and the *choice* actions were given in speedcode, earlier (see Chapter 1). Now all we need in order to make these blocks useful is a streamlining technique for producing kludgecode.

The streamlined version of *choice* action is given in both 8080 and 6800 kludgecode, below.

```
CHOICE ACTION (speedcode)
    if (predicate) then
                        LABEL 1:
                        else
                        LABEL 2:
        end if
end CHOICE ACTION


CHOICE ACTION (6800 kludgecode)
*   process predicate like an expression
            CMP                 **compare to set condition codes
            Bxy LABEL 2         **branch depending on condition code
        LABEL 1 _____
                _____
                _____
                _____
            BRA ENDIF     **skip over else clause
        LABEL 2 _____
                _____
                _____
                _____
        ENDIF             **done
    end CHOICE ACTION
```

As an example of 6800 kludgecode in action, suppose we split the flow of control in a program by testing the value of variable X.

```
if (X = 0) then
        YES:  Y:= (X + 5);
        else
        NO:   Y:= 0;
end if
```

The kludgecode for this branch is produced according to the SESE requirement. Every time the **if** is executed, it terminates at the same place: **endif.**

```
            LDA   A   X
            CMP   A   #0
            BNE       NO          **branch on the negative of =
YES         LDA   A   X
            ADD   A   #5
            STA   A   Y           **Y:= (X + 5)
            BRA       ENDIF       **always skip over
*           the else clause goes here
NO          LDA   A   #0
            STA   A   Y           **Y:= 0
ENDIF       _____
            _____
            _____
```

It is extremely important to notice how the BNE instruction was obtained above. In every case of an if predicate, we perform the test (CMP) and then branch according to the opposite condition indicated (the opposite of zero is nonzero). Thus, if the speedcode uses some *Boolean logic* operation BOOL, we must branch on the condition NOT BOOL. The example below illustrates this in more detail.

```
if (Y < X + Z) then
        LESS:   _____
                _____
                _____

        else
        MORE:   _____
                _____
end if          _____
```

This is streamlined into kludgecode for the 6800 and 8080 microprocessors as follows.

```
6800 KLUDGECODE
*         (Y < X + Z)
            LDA   A   X
            LDA   B   Z
            ABA   B               **(X + Z)
            PSH   A               **save (X + Z) on TOS
            LDA   A   Y           **get Y
            PUL   B               **(X + Z) in ACCB
            CBA                   **Y is compared with (X + Z)
            BGE       MORE        **branch on greater or equal
```

```
*            then clause
LESS         _____
             _____
             _____

*            BRA      END IF     **skip over
MORE         _____               **the else clause
             _____
             _____
ENDIF                            **done with both
end 6800 KLUDGECODE
```

The choice action is implemented in 8080 kludgecode by observing the differences between these two microprocessors. These were pointed out in the previous section. We must work around the limited access to the registers and stack, and in this illustration we use two 8080 instructions to accomplish the equivalent of BGE.

```
8080 KLUDGECODE
                   LDA    X
                   MOV    B, A       **put X in ACC B
                   LDA    Z
                   ADD    B          **(X + Z) in ACC A
                   MOV    B, A       **bypass the stack
                   LDA    Y          **get Y in ACC A
                   CMP    B          **compare Y: (X + Z)
                   JZ     MORE       **equal to or
                   JP     MORE       **greater than (JPE)
          then clause
LESS               _____
                   _____
                   _____
                   JMP END IF        **skip to END IF
*         else clause
MORE               _____
                   _____
                   _____
ENDIF              _____            **done
end 8080 KLUDGECODE
```

The predicate evaluation performed in each CHOICE ACTION is slightly different than the assignment statement evaluation. We can generalize the predicate expression as shown in the next illustration. Suppose we streamline the following:

```
if ((X + 5) > (Y — S/Z)) then
                    DO: _____
                        _____
                        _____
                    else
                    DON'T: _____
                           _____
                           _____
end if
```

```
6800 KLUDGECODE
*        (X + 5) > (Y — S/Z)
            LDA    A    X
            ADD    A    #5
            PSH    A                    **save (X + 5) on TOS
*
            LDA    A    Y
            PSH    A
            LDA    A    S
            PSH    A
            LDA    A    Z
            PSH    A
            JSR         DIV             **(S/Z)
            PUL    B                    **quotient (S/Z)
            PUL    A                    **discard remainder (S/Z)
            PUL    A                    **get Y, now
            SBA                         **Y — S/Z in ACC A
            PSH    A                    **now on TOS
*
*        do comparisons
*           PUL    B
            PUL    A
            CBA                         **compare (X + 5):(Y — S/Z)
            BLE         DON'T           **skip to else clause
DO          _____
            _____
            _____
            BRA         END IF          **skip over else clause
DON'T       _____
            _____
            _____
END IF      _____                      **done
            _____

end 6800 KLUDGECODE
```

The kludgecode above employs a DIV routine. The DIV procedure accepts two numbers from the TOS and does the divide in integer arithmetic. The result is a quotient and remainder. The quotient is pulled first, then the remainder. In this example we had no use for the remainder, so it was discarded by PUL A, PUL A as shown. The first PUL copied the remainder, while the second PUL wiped it out and replaced it with the value of Y.

The final important building block is the looping action. Recall its general form:

```
while (predicate) loop;
            _____
            _____
            _____
end loop;
```

The 8080 kludgecode for the simple counting loop below shows how simple it is to produce looping programs.

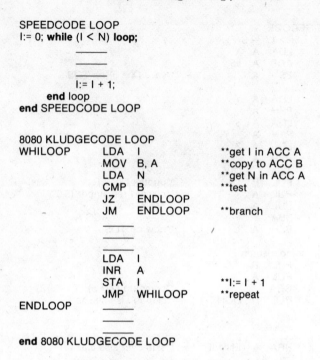

```
SPEEDCODE LOOP
I:= 0; while (I < N) loop;
        _____
        _____
        _____
        I:= I + 1;
    end loop
end SPEEDCODE LOOP


8080 KLUDGECODE LOOP
WHILOOP      LDA    I            **get I in ACC A
             MOV    B, A         **copy to ACC B
             LDA    N            **get N in ACC A
             CMP    B            **test
             JZ     ENDLOOP
             JM     ENDLOOP      **branch
             _____
             _____
             LDA    I
             INR    A
             STA    I            **I:= I + 1
             JMP    WHILOOP      **repeat
ENDLOOP      _____
             _____

end 8080 KLUDGECODE LOOP
```

In a sense, the **while** loop is a composite of an **if** and **goto**. For example, we can imagine the equivalence of the two as follows.

$$\text{while} \quad \equiv \quad \text{if ( ) then ... goto} \quad \text{else ...}$$

In a similar manner, the **until** loop is a composite of the **if** and **goto**. This is shown below.

$$\text{until} \quad \equiv \quad \text{..... if ( ) then ...} \quad \text{else goto}$$

The problem with these equivalent forms is that they open the door to proliferation of **goto**'s. This would violate the goto rule, and lead to undisciplined (non-SESE) programs. Thus, the *looping* statements provide a convenient and safe mechanism for programmers.

A simple loop is implemented in kludgecode in a simple streamlining operation. Thus, in many instances the 6800 kludgecode will resemble the form below (no use of the stack).

```
while (I ≤ N) loop  ...  end loop
WLOOP        LDA    A   I
             LDA    B   N
             CBA                 **N:I
             BGT    ENDLOOP      **skip when done
             _____
             _____
```

```
                BRA      WLOOP       **repeat
ENDLOOP         ____
                ____
```

The 6800 kludgecoder should also remember that the BRA instruction uses the short relative addressing format. When long loops are implemented, it may be necessary to use the long address format JMP WLOOP.

An **until** loop is often more convenient to use in kludgecode programs. Thus the streamlined **until** loop for the 6800 kludgecode is given for future reference.

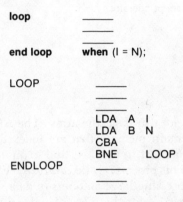

```
loop              ____
                  ____

end loop        when (I = N);

LOOP              ____
                  ____
                  ____
                  LDA   A   I
                  LDA   B   N
                  CBA
                  BNE       LOOP
ENDLOOP           ____
                  ____
```

We are finally in a position to write all programs. This startling fact is demonstrated in the following section. The remaining chapters will, in fact, use the three structures over and over again: *basic* actions, *choice* actions, *looping* actions. Only cleverness and intelligence stands between the kludgecode programmer and successful system implementations that employ the Electrifying, Streamlined Blueprint Speedcode Method!

Some Useful Kludgecode

We have claimed that any program can be written with three simple building blocks. We have also insisted that the methodology advocated in this book leads to successful systems. The basis for these outrageous claims are given by the chapter titles: "Never Write A Large Program," "Program In Levels Of Abstraction," etc. Suppose we begin to apply these concepts to useful situations.

Suppose we desire a subprocedure to sum the elements of an array (block of contiguous memory bytes). We can imagine using a *looping* action to repeatedly add to a running total, SUM. The speedcode for such a procedure appears as follows.

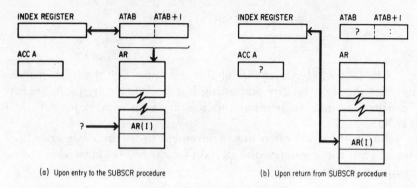

(a) Upon entry to the SUBSCR procedure   (b) Upon return from SUBSCR procedure

Fig. 4.1 The subscript operator.

```
SUM:= 0;
I:= 0; while (I < N) loop;
     SUM:= SUM + AR(I);
     I:= I + 1;
     end loop;
```

This routine introduces a new idea in data: the array. The AR(I) structure is a collection of bytes in main memory that are indexed by variable I. When I is zero, the first byte of AR is accessed, and so on until the last value AR(N — 1) is accessed. This process is called *array indexing*, and is a very useful technique for processing large amounts of data.

If we attempt to generate kludgecode for the piece of code, above, we quickly learn that the subscripted array AR causes complexity we are not equipped to handle. How can we overcome the subscript problem?

The solution is to use levels of abstraction. We will create a subscripting subprocedure that computes the address of AR(I), given the address of AR, and the value of I. The convention used to do this is shown in Fig. 4.1.

We use the *index register* of most microprocessors to point to the array element we want to access. This approach is implemented on the 6800 by using the IX register for indexing. On the 8080 architecture we employ the HL-pair for indexing. In either case we use the index register as a *pointer* to the data.

Upon entry to subprocedure SUBSCR, we must guarantee that the index register points to a word in memory that holds the address of AR. This word is called ATAB, but of course it can be any word selected by the calling program. Also, the accumulator register is set-up with the value of subscript I. This value is added to the stored in ATAB to arrive at the address of the value stored in AR(I).

Upon exit from the subprocedure SUBSER, we find the address of AR(I) in the index register. This will allow access by way of indexed addressing on the 6800, or by way of memory referencing in the 8080.

Since the ATAB word in memory is modified, we must restore it to the address of the array before calling SUBSCR, again. This is illustrated in the calling sequence given below in kludgecode-6800.

```
*  Calling sequence for SUBSCR
        LDX       #AR          **address of AR
        STX       ATAB         **set up ATAB
        LDX       #ATAB        **point to ATAB
        LDA   A   I            **set up index in A
        JSR       SUBSCR       **compute address of AR(I)
```

This sequence produces the result shown in Fig. 4.1b. In the following kludgecode for the summation routine, we see how the I-th element of a table is accessed after the calling sequence is executed.

```
BLUE₂: 6800 kludgecode
*  SUM:= 0
                LDA   A   #0
                STA   A   SUM
*  I:= 0
                LDA   A   #0
                STA   A   I
*  WHILE LOOP
                LDA   A   I
                LDA   B   N
                CBA
                BGE       EWHILE       **skip if I ≥ N
*  SUM:= SUM + AR(I)
                LDA   A   SUM
                PSH   A
*  calling sequence
                LDX       #AR
                STX       ATAB
                LDX       #ATAB
                LDA   A   I
                JSR       SUBSCR
*  SUM + AR(I)
                PUL   B                **SUM is in ACCB
                LDA   A   0, X         **use IX to get AR(I)
                ABA                    **SUM + AR(I) in ACCA
                STA   A   SUM          **:=
*  I:= I + 1
                LDA   A   I
                INC   A                **increment instruction
                STA   A   I            **I:=
*  END LOOP
                BRA       WLOOP        **repeat loop
        EWHILE  _____
                _____
                _____
end BLUE₂
```

The equivalent kludgecode for the 8080 is straightforward by substitution. It is left as an exercise for the reader. The real mystery, however, is how the SUBSCR routine works. This is explained, briefly, in blueprint form.

BLUE₀: SUBSCR Routine
    1. Use the index register to obtain the address of the array.
    2. Add the 16-bit index register to the 8-bit accumulator (I), and be sure
       to carry the carry bit forward.
    3. Beware of condition code settings when loading, storing, adding, etc.
end BLUE₀

With this advice in mind, we will write a speedcode routine to do
the addition. This is done in a variety of ways, but they all lead to a brief
program similar to the one shown below. We have left the speedcode
level to the reader.

BLUE₂: SUBSCR Routine

```
SUBSCR      INX                  **fetch ATAB + 1 byte
            CLC                  **clear carry flag
            ADD   A   0, X       **add together; AR + i
            STA   A   0, X       **save in ATAB + 1
            DEX                  **get ATAB, next
            LDA   A   #0         **prepare to add in C bit
            ADC   A   0, X       **add high order byte
*    we have just computed: #0 + (A) + (C)
            STA   A   0, X       **put back into ATAB
            LDX       0, X       **put address in X
            RTS                  **return
end BLUE₂
```

The reader may still be mystified by the SUBSCR routine. Therefore, study the step-by-step execution of this routine in Fig. 4.2. Suppose
the main memory locations are given as below:

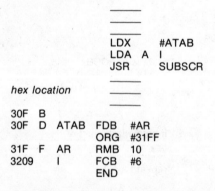

```
                    LDX      #ATAB
                    LDA  A   I
                    JSR      SUBSCR

hex location        ____

30F  B
30F  D   ATAB   FDB   #AR
                ORG   #31FF
31F  F   AR     RMB   10
3209     I      FCB   #6
                END
```

We can use this piece of code to explain the results of Fig. 4.2. The
operation is done to locate AR(6).

In Fig. 4.2a the JSR is executed passing the values of C, ACCA, IX,
and ATAB as shown. Note that 30FD is the *address* of ATAB, while the
value of ATAB is 31FF. In turn, the value of ATAB is the address of array
AR. The array is 10 bytes long, beginning at location 31FF. These num-

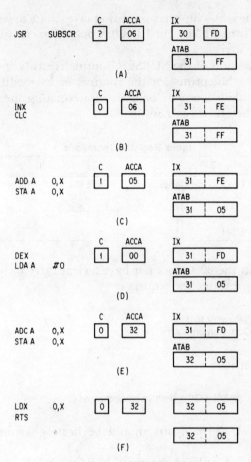

Fig. 4.2 SUBSCR execution.

bers have been chosen to exercise all that we know about the process being demonstrated. There is no special reason to locate the array AR at this place in memory.

At point b, (see Fig. 4.2) the index register has been bumped up to point to the least significant byte of ATAB. This is done so we can add the value stored in ACCA to the value stored in the low-order byte of IX. This snapshot also shows the effect of clearing the carry bit, CLC.

In step c we performed the addition (FF) + (06) = (05) and set C = 1. Thus the carry-out is kept in register C until we are able to add it to the most-significant byte of the ATAB pointer.

Step d adjusts the index register to point to the most-significant byte of ATAB. It also prepares the ACCA to add the carry bit, only. But because we must include the ACCA in the addition, we must clear A without destroying the value in C.

Finally, the add-with-carry operation takes place and the new index value is copied into ATAB. The LDX 0,X operation completes the necessary processing steps.

An 8080 version of the SUBSCR routine is easily implemented by streamlining the blueprints for the routine, or by modifying the 6800 version. The table below may be useful for equating the IX register in the 6800 with the HL register in the 8080.

Index Register Operations

8080		6800	
LHLD	label	LDX	label
INX	H	INX	
DCX	H	DEX	
POP	H		
PUSH	H		

In addition the 8080 does not have a clear carry instruction, so we would have to substitute the sequence:

```
STC        Set carry to 1
CMC        Complement carry
```

or else use subterfuge:

```
ANA   A       AND ACCA with itself and clear C
```

These kludgecode shenanigans should be heavily documented in the SUBSCR routine.

As a final example of the three building blocks, we explore the inner workings of a simple multiply routine. Suppose we design this routine to work on small integers (8-bits each) and to produce a small result (8-bit result). We could use the basic routine to do 16-bit multiply with some modification, but instead we will return the largest possible 8-bit integer in the event that the result overflows.

The routine is passed two one-byte integers via the stack, produces a product, and returns the value PROD via the stack. A speedcode version appears below.

```
BLUE₁: MULTIPLY
MULT: procedure (M1: tos byte, MO: tos byte)
          var SIGN    : byte;
          var PROD    : byte;
          var COUNT : byte;
          var AMT      : byte;
          ;
          SIGN:= 1   ;
```

```
            PROD:= 0     ;
            ;
            COUNT:= M1;
            if (COUNT < 0) then
                        FLIP: SIGN:= COMP (SIGN);
                              COUNT:= COMP (COUNT);
                        end if;
            AMT:= MO;
            if (AMT < 0) then
                        FLOP: SIGN:= COMP (SIGN);
                              AMT:= COMP (AMT);
                        end if;
            while (COUNT > 0) loop;
                  PROD:= PROD + AMT: OVERFLOW
                  if OVERFLOW then
                                BIG: PROD:= 127;
                                     exit loop;
                  COUNT:= COUNT — 1;
            end loop;
            ;
            if (SIGN < 0) then
                        NEG: PROD:= COMP (PROD);
            return (PROD: TOS BYTE);
            ;
      end MULT
      end BLUE₁
```

We only sketch the kludgecode for this multiply routine since the reader can easily complete the kludgecode streamlining from the following. First, the return address must be saved, since the values passed to this procedure are on the TOS. (We skip over the RMBs for data.)

```
*               PROCEDURE
MULT            PUL   A
                STA   A ⎤ ← save
                PUL   A ⎥
                STA   A ⎦ ← save + 1
*               SIGN:= 1; PROD:= 0;
*               (left to reader)
*               COUNT:= M1;
                PUL   A                    **get M1 from TOS
                STA   A   COUNT            **COUNT:=
                LDA   A   COUNT            **get it, again
                LDA   B   #0               **get zero
                CBA
                BGE   FLIPOUT              **skip over
FLIP            LDA   A   SIGN             **get COMP of SIGN
                NEG   A                    **two's complement in 6800
                STA   A   SIGN             **SIGN:=
*               COMP (COUNT)
                LDA   A   COUNT
                NEG   A
                STA   A   COUNT            **COUNT:= COMP (COUNT)
*               NO ELSE clause
FLIPOUT         PUL   A                    **get M0
                STA   A   AMT              **AMT:= M0
*               (reader can do this) if (AMT > 0) then . . .
```

```
*              while (COUNT > 0) loop
WLOOP          LDA  A  COUNT
               LDA  B  #0
               CBA
               BLE     END LOOP        **COUNT ≤ 0?
*              "body of loop"
               LDA  A  PROD
               PSH  A
               LDA  A  AMT
               PUL  B  PROD
               ABA                     **PROD + AMT
*              now test IF (OVERFLOW) with BVS in 6800
               BVS     BIG             **yes, overflow
               BRA     NOBIG           **no, skip
BIG            LDA  A  #127
               STA  A  PROD            **PROD:= 127
               JMP     END LOOP2       **EXITLOOP
NOBIG          LDA  A  COUNT
               DEC  A
               STA  A  COUNT           **COUNT:= COUNT + 1
*              END LOOP (end of loop)
END LOOP2      LDA  A  SIGN
               LDA  B  #0
               CBA                     **SIGN 0?
               BGE     NOTNEG          **no
*              NEG: PROD:= COMP (PROD)
*              (left for reader)
*              RETURN (PROD: TOSBYTE)
NOTNEG         LDA  A  PROD
               PSH  A                  **pass via TOS
               LDA  A  SAVE + 1
               PSH  A
               LDA  A  SAVE
               PSH  A                  **return address on TOS
               RTS
*              END
               END
```

The moderate size of this routine illustrates how it is possible to write large amounts of code in kludgecode language, but never have to write a large segment of code at once. Each statement of speedcode can be *independently* streamlined into kludgecode.

The resultant kludgecode will be less efficient than a directly coded program. This is evident in several places in the multiply procedure. But remember, the object is to get it working correctly first, and then make it fast. Indeed, we can make the multiply routine correct *and* fast by employing a final level of streamlining. This is done in the next chapter.

5
Make It Faster
After You Make It Work!

Rocketboy Roger was a daring race car driver. He drove in destruction derbies; he was fearless as a stock car ace. His future was bright, and his income looking up when he bought his first classic auto.

Rocketboy nearly made it to the top, but he lacked precision. In every race he sped to the front of the line of competitors and stayed there throughout the race. Eventually, he would take one chance too many and crash, blow-up the engine, or run out of gasoline too soon. His sponsors always believed he would win, but he never did.

The fans loved Rocketboy. He gave them the thrills they came to see. His daring, speed, and risky driving brought the grandstands to the edge of shrieking ecstacy.

But eventually Rocketboy faded into history. He could no longer interest car owners in his feats of daring. They all knew Rocketboy would tear up their cars and never win a race. Rocketboy simply could not resist the temptation to go fast, before he knew where he was going.

* * *

Seething Kludgecode Shorthand

Nearly every microprocessor has a collection of addressing modes or operations designed to increase the efficiency of the processor. These codes and modes take the form of special instructions and assembler directed addressing modes.

We can take advantage of the special instructions and the special addressing modes when streamlining the kludgecode of a microprocessor program. However, we must be careful to avoid tricks which will lead to unreadable code, or unreliable practices. The added speed of processing may not be worth the cost of program debugging and maintenance.

For example, the following table illustrates a few instructions taken from 8080 and 6800 kludgecode sets that use *immediate addressing* to shorten the length of the instruction (and in some cases the time to execute the instruction).

53

Immediate Addressing

8080		6800		
SUI	constant	SUB	reg	# const
ADI	constant	ADD	reg	# const
LXI	double reg, constant	LDA	reg	# const
MVI	reg, constant	LDA	reg	# const
CPI	constant	CMP	reg	# const

We have used this mode in many places to improve the 6800 kludge-code. We could improve it even further using the following special instructions and addressing modes for streamlining speedcode.

EXAMPLES

Speedcode	8080		6800	
PROD:= 0;	MVI	A, 00H	CLR	PROD
	STA	PROD		
PROD:= 1;	MVI	A, 01H	CLR	PROD
	STA	PROD	INC	PROD
PROD:= —1;	MVI	A, FFH	CLR	PROD
	STA	PROD	DEC	PROD
I:= I + 1;	LDA	I	INC	I
	INR	A		
	STA	I		
I:= I —1;	LDA	I	DEC	I
	DCR	A		
	STA	I		

END EXAMPLES

The kludgecode of a particular program development can be streamlined even further by using the special operations and addressing modes provided in most microprocessors. When we reduce the length of a program in this manner we call the resultant code *flashcode*.

Flashcode is optimized kludgecode. It is optimized to reduce program length and program running time.

There are no clear-cut rules for when to use flashcode shorthand, and this is the reason it may lead to poor program composition. If we make the programs correct before we make them faster, we can avoid many of the errors that result when programmers take advantage of machine-dependent features. Therefore, in the examples to follow, we must be careful about how kludgecode is modified in the interest of speed.

Take a Chemist to Lunch

The chemist's problem of Chapter 2 can be used to illustrate the efficiency gained by streamlining kludgecode into flashcode. First, we write the kludgecode of the speedcode given in Chapter 2. Then, we can study the kludgecode for opportunities to make it faster and/or shorter.

We recall each speedcode line, one at a time. In the 6800 kludgecode version, we have rigorously followed the rules for reliable streamlining.

BLUE₂: Chemist's Problem

```
*     I:= I + 1
            LDA   A   I
            PSH   A                 **stack I
            LDA   A   #1
            PSH   A                 **stack #1
            PUL   B                 **get #1 back
            PUL   A                 **get I back
            ABA                     **I + 1
            STA   A   I             **I:=
*     SELECT: case FLAG of;
            LDA   A   FLAG
            CMP   A   #0
            BNE       ONE
*     "0": DI:= INPUT
            JSR   INPUT             **input to ACC A
            LDA   A   #1
            STA   A   FLAG          **FLAG:= 1
            RTS                     **return
*     "1": DIFFI:= INPUT — DI
            CMP   A   #1
            BNE       TWO
            JSR       INPUT         **number in ACC A
            PSH   A                 **save on TOS
            LDI   A   DI
            PSH   A
            PUL   B
            PUL   A
            SBA                     **INPUT — DI
            STA   A   DIFFI         **DIFFI:=
*     FLAG:= 2
            LDA   A
            PSH   A
            PUL   A
            STA   A   FLAG          **FLAG:= 2
            RTS
*     "2": DI:= INPUT
            CMP   A   #3
            BNE       THREE
            JSR       INPUT         **get number in ACC A
            STA   A   DI            **DI:=
            LDA   A   #3
            STA   A   FLAG          **FLAG:= 3
            RTS
*     "3": DIFFI:= INPUT — DI
            CMP   A   #3
            BNE       FINISH        **none of the above
            JSR       INPUT         **number into ACC A
            PSH   A                 **save on TOS
            LDA   A   DI
            PSH   A                 **save DI on TOS
```

```
                PUL  B                      **get DI back
                PUL  A                      **get number back
                SBA                         **INPUT — DI
                STA  A   DIFFI              **DIFFI:=
SIGNAL          LDA  A   SLOPE
                CMP  A   #—1                **which case is it?
                BNE      ZERO
*       "1": IF (. . .)
                LDA  A   THRESH
                LDA  B   DIFFI
                CBA                         **DIFFI < THRESH?
                BGE      ENDIF1             **no
                LDA  A   THRESH
                LDA  B   DIFFI1
                CBA
                BGE      ENDIF1             **DIFFI1 < THRESH?
                LDA  A   THRESH
                NEG  A                      **—THRESH
                LDA  B   DIFFI
                CBA
                BLE      ENDIF1             **DIFFI > —THRESH?
                LDA  A   THRESH
                NEG  A
                LDA  B   DIFFI1
                CBA
                BLE      ENDIF1             **skip if clause
OUTS            LDA  A   #0
                STA  A   SLOPE              **SLOPE:= 0
                LDA  A   I                  **parameter in ACC A
                JSR      STOP               **call STOP
ENDIF1          RTS                         **return
*
*       "0": IF (. . .)
*       (this is left to the reader to complete)
*
end BLUE₂
```

The speedcode-to-kludgecode streamlined program can easily be completed in a straightforward manner. Each line of speedcode is converted, blindly, into kludgecode. In the process, however, many shortouts were noted.

Let us review the kludgecode for the chemist's problem, and develop a flashcode version. In the following we display the flashcode on the left-hand side, along with the previously developed kludgecode placed on the right-hand side.

```
BLUE₃: Flashcode
*       I:= I + 1
        INC   I                    **LDA AI; PSH A; LDA A #1; PSH A;
                                   **PUL B; PUL A; ABA; STA I
*       select:  case FLAG of;
        TST      FLAG              **LDA A FLAG; CMP A #0;
        BNE      ONE               **DNE ONE
*       "0":  DI:= INPUT
```

```
              JSR         INPUT          **JSR INPUT
              STA    A    DI             **STA A DI
              CLR         FLAG           **LDA A #1
              INC         FLAG           **STA A FLAG
              RTS                        **RTS
*   "1": DIFFI:= INPUT — DI
              LDA    A    FLAG 7         **CMP A #1
              CMP    A    #1             **BNE TWO
              BNE         TWO
              JSR         INPUT          **JSR INPUT
              LDA    B    DI             **PSH A; LDA A; PSH A;
              SBA                        **PUL B; PUL A; SBA
              STA    A    DIFFI          **STA * DIFFI
*   FLAG:= 2;
              CLR         FLAG           **LDA A #2
              INC         FLAG           **PSH A
              INC         FLAG           **PUL A; STA A FLAG
              RTS                        **RTS
```

This code is continued; at each section where we can optimize the sequence of kludgecode statements we do so. In the compound predicate of the **if** statement, we save a number of steps by noting the redundant LDA and STA operations.

```
*   "—1": IF (. . .)
              LDA    A    THRESH         **LDA A THRESH
              LDA    B    DIFFI          **LDA B DIFFI
              CBA                        **CBA
              BGE         ENDIF1         **BGE ENDIF1
              LDA    B    DIFFI          **LDA A THRESH; LDA B DIFFI
              CBA                        **CBA
              BGE         ENDIF1         **BGE ENDIF1
              NEG    A                   **LDA A THRESH; NEG A
              LDA    B    DIFFI          **LDA A DIFFI
              CBA                        **CBA
              BLE         ENDIF1         **BLE ENDIF1
              LDA    B    DIFFI1         **LDA A THRESH; NEG A;
              CBA                        **LDA B DIFFI1; CBA
              BLE         ENDIF1         **BLE ENDIF1
              CLR         SLOPE          **LDA A #0; STA A SLOPE
              LDA    A    I              **LDA A I
              JSR         STOP           **JSR   STOP
              RTS                        **RTS
ENDIF1
```

The thorough application of flashcode optimization can save from 10% to 80% in the size of programs. It is necessary to emphasize, however, that the application of code optimization to kludgecode is a process that can be carried to extremes. The overall goal of streamlining is to produce less costly software. The cost of software must include the maintenance costs as well. Thus programs must remain readable.

From Speedcode to Flashcode

There are few reliable rules for producing flashcode given a program in speedcode. We have employed a couple of simple guidelines in the previous examples, but large savings in memory space and execution time require painstaking labor which may not be worth a programmer's effort for the overall result. Several guidelines used are listed below:

1. Combine STA LDA sequences that are found back-to-back. For example, we discovered sequences that wasted memory and speed in the chemist's example.

```
LDA   A   FLAG
STA   A   FLAG
LDA   A   FLAG
```

2. Make use of time-saving instructions and addressing modes in the kludgecode.

```
LDA   A   #0
STA   A   COUNT
```

This can be replaced by

```
CLR      COUNT
```

In many cases, loops use an increment to increase the loop counter.

```
I:=  I + 1;
```

When this is done, we can directly increment I using 6800 kludgecode.

```
INC      I
```

This form is much more efficient than the straightforward method for assignment;

```
LDA   A   I
LDA   B   #1
ABA
STA   A   I
```

3. Eliminate repeated segments of code by subprocedures and careful planning.

4. Factor out redundant LDA instructions as illustrated in the chemist's problem.

5. Use common sense.

The optimization of kludgecode is a process so dependent on the architecture that the skills needed to do it must be acquired by experience.

In the following chapters we develop many program modules that add to the programmer's experience in programming microprocessors of the 8080 and 6800 type. These tools will most likely be available in the system software of the particular microprocessor. That is, they are so common that nearly every system is delivered fully equipped with them. It is often instructive, however, to reinvent software wheels in order to understand how they work.

6
Reinventing the Software Wheels

When I was in school, I worked in a gasoline service station. Every-day or two an old man would pull up next to the Regular pump and ask for one dollar's worth of petrol. One day I asked the old man why he drove such an old car (his car was a splendid 1934 Buick). I was assuming he had antique automobiles in mind, but instead, he said he simply liked the old automobile better than the new ones.

As the years passed by, I often saw the old man in his old car. The man and the car began to show their age, and one day I stopped them in a parking lot to ask why he did not retire the dilapidated car. He said he was going to drive it forever because he couldn't find a suitable sub-stitute. He said his obsession stemmed from the comfort he felt with the old car. "I can't understand how these new-fangled cars work, but this old Buick is simple to fix, easy to run, and unsophisticated, like me," he exclaimed as he opened the rusted door.

* * *

Software Wheels

Every computer uses a collection of very basic routines to perform mundane tasks such as input and output of characters, number conver-sion, and general housekeeping chores. In most microprocessor systems, these fundamental routines must be reinvented, borrowed, or purchased for a particular architecture.

In this chapter we develop blueprints for several of the most com-mon routines used in microcomputing. We call them *software wheels*, because in a broad sense we are reinventing the programs that are com-monly available on most computer systems. Indeed, they may be avail-able in the particular microprocessor development system employed by the reader.

It is instructive to understand how the fundamental routines work. They reveal the inner workings of the microprocessor that executes them, and they provide an opportunity to study technique. For these reasons we will reinvent several software wheels for the reader to study.

The first spoke in the microprocessor software wheel is INBYTE and OUTCHAR. The INBYTE routine accepts a character in ASCII code from a keyboard, and OUTCHAR sends a character out to a video screen, for example. The most important process in these two routines is illustrated in the blueprint for INBYTE.

BLUE$_0$: INBYTE
1. There are two phases in byte I/O dealing with a status register called IOSTAT, and a data transfer register called IODATA.
2. In phase I, we test the status register to determine if an incoming character is ready to be copied into the processor's memory (working register ACCA, for example). If *not* ready, we repeat this step.
3. If step two detects a ready condition in the IOSTAT register, then we can transmit a character. Thus, the second phase is to copy a character from IODATA to the ACCA register.

End BLUE$_0$

Thus, the two most important actions carried out by an I/O routine like INBYTE are (a) waiting and testing, and (b) copying the available byte from its register into a microprocessor register. With some added effort, we can design a simple INBYTE routine in speedcode.

```
BLUE₁: Speedcode for INBYTE
INBYTE: procedure (  );
        const      STATUS : byte = #IOSTAT;
        const      DATA   : byte = #IODATA;
        var        CHAR   : byte
        ;
        PHASE 1: loop end loop when (STATUS = RDY);
        PHASE 2: CHAR:= DATA;

        ;
        return (CHAR: ACCA);
    end INBYTE
    end BLUE₁
```

The speedcode version of INBYTE may look strange at first glance. The **loop end loop** statement does nothing except repeatedly test the status register of the microprocessor interface to the device. Thus the status and data constants are actually locations in the microprocessor's address space that turn out to be special-purpose registers for holding input/output status and data. This form of I/O is called *memory mapped I/O*.

The 6800 kludgecode for the INBYTE routine is straightforward per the streamlined speedcode.

```
BLUE₂: 6800 kludgecode
INBYTE
RDY        EQU        #$01
```

```
STATUS   EQU       #IOSTAT
DATA     EQU       #IODATA
CHAR     RMB       1
LOOP1    LDA   A   STATUS      **LOOP ...
         CMP   A   RDY         **END LOOP
         BNE       LOOP1       **UNTIL (STATUS = RDY)
 *
         LDA   A   DATA
         STA   A   CHAR        **CHAR:= DATA
 *
         LDA   A   CHAR
         RTS                   **return (CHAR: ACCA)
CHAR     RMB       1
end BLUE₂
```

This routine is streamlined even further by resorting to flashcode techniques. For example, the redundant LDA and STA operations on CHAR can be omitted now that we fully comprehend the process. The flashcode version of INBYTE gives another level of abstraction. (The TST instruction sets the zero condition flag if the result of a comparison is zero.)

```
BLUE₃: 6800 flashcode
INBYTE
RDY      EQU       #01         **the RDY flag is 01 when ready
STATUS   EQU       #IOSTAT     **the value of IOSTAT is machine
                                 dependent
DATA     EQU       #IODATA     **the value of IODATA is machine
                                 dependent
 *
LOOP1    TST       STATUS      **is it zero?
         BEQ       LOOP1       **yes, try again; no, go on
 *
         LDA   A   DATA        **phase two
         RTS                   **return (ACCA)
end BLUE₃
```

Note in the routine above, we did not directly use RDY. In general, the condition flag may be #$01 or it may be some other value. If the flag changes value we may not be able to use the TST instruction in place of the LDA and CMP pair of instructions. Furthermore, the status and data locations may change from one microprocessor to another. These values must be carefully checked (they may be selectable by moving small jumper pins).

The next useful software wheel is the OUTCHAR routine. This routine will copy the contents of ACCA to the data location when the status register indicates that the output device is ready. The speedcode version of OUTCHAR shows once again the important two phases.

```
BLUE₁: Speedcode for OUTCHAR
        OUTCHAR: procedure (CHAR: ACCA);
                 const       STATUS : BYTE = #IOSTAT;
```

```
const         DATA    : BYTE = #IODATA;
;
PHASE 1: loop end loop when (STATUS = RDY);
PHASE 2: DATA:= CHAR;
return
     end OUTCHAR;
end BLUE₁
```

The reader can easily produce kludgecode and in turn flashcode for this routine. In the 8080 microprocessor we must be careful to move the output character to register B while the status loop is executing. This is a necessity because the A register is used to communicate directly with the status register of the device. The 8080 flashcode for OUTCHAR will look like the following.

```
OUTCHAR
          MOV     B, A       **save CHAR in B
LOOP      IN      0          **get status byte in A
          ANI     RDY        **logically AND A with RDY
          JZ      LOOP       **try again if zero result
          MOV     A, B       **restore CHAR in A
          OUT     0          **output to device zero
          RET                **return
```

The 6800 and 8080 routines both perform two phases during input and output. They may require slightly different programming style, but the principle remains the same. Also note how helpful the speedcode version is *regardless of the architecture being used by the coder.*

The next challenge confronting the pioneering microprocessor programmer is the conversion of ASCII code into decimal numbers. Recall the ASCII code for numerals:

ASCII Hexadecimal	Numeral
30	0
31	1
32	2
33	3
34	4
35	5
36	6
37	7
38	8
39	9

This code shows the form of an input or output character when transmitted by INBYTE or OUTCHAR. The machine uses binary, however, and so we must be able to get from an ASCII string to a single binary number.

Suppose we input and store the ASCII string 53 in the memory of a microprocessor. The actual storage locations will contain two bytes of binary encoded ASCII: 3533_{16}. These two bytes must be converted into a single binary number: 110101_2.

The algorithm for performing the decoding and compression of an ASCII string into a single binary number is developed in levels of abstraction. The blueprints are self-explanatory.

BLUE$_0$: BINARY
1. Given the address of a line of ASCII numerals, convert them into a 8-bit, binary number.
2. Use the "shift and add" method of conversion. That is, multiply the running sum by 10, add the next significant digit to the running sum, and continue this until no further digits need to be converted.
3. Return the 8-bit decimal (binary) number to the calling routine by way of the accumulator.

end BLUE$_0$

The shift and add algorithm is simply a method of adding the units, tens, hundreds, etc. Suppose the number to be converted is an ASCII encoded string:

$$158$$

The method used in the algorithm begins with the most significant decimal digit:

$$TOTAL = 1$$

Then, the total is shifted by multiplication, so the next digit can be added.

$$TOTAL = 1 * 10 + 5$$

This total is again shifted so we can add the final digit.

$$total = 15 * 10 + 8$$
$$= 150 + 8$$
$$= 158$$

Along the way, we must strip off the ASCII encoding. This is done by subtracting the hexadecimal "zone" from each numeral. Thus, 8 is obtained in binary form by subtracting 30_{16} from 8.

BLUE$_1$: Speedcode for BINARY

```
BINARY: procedure      (@LINE: accx)
        var            DECNUM : byte;
        var            LINE   : byte;
        const          HEX    : byte ≠ $30;
        ;
        DECNUM:= 0; while (@LINE = CR) loop;
                    DECNUM:= 10 * DECNUM + (@LINE — HEX);
                    LINE:= LINE + 1;
                    end loop;
        return (DECNUM : acca)
    end BINARY
end BLUE₁
```

The speedcode version of BINARY passes the address (pointer) of the ASCII string by way of the index register ACCX. This is indicated by the indirect address operator @. In the body of the **while** loop the address is used as a pointer, and later as a value. When the address is incremented, we have used LINE as a value.

The 6800 flashcode for this program is a straightforward streamlining job. It does illustrate, however, how to use the index register.

BLUE₂: Flashcode for BINARY

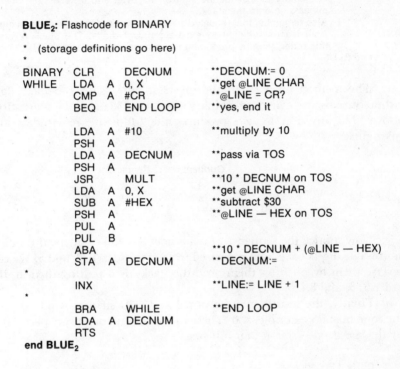

```
*
*    (storage definitions go here)
*
BINARY   CLR       DECNUM        **DECNUM:= 0
WHILE    LDA   A   0, X          **get @LINE CHAR
         CMP   A   #CR           **@LINE = CR?
         BEQ       END LOOP      **yes, end it
*
         LDA   A   #10           **multiply by 10
         PSH   A
         LDA   A   DECNUM        **pass via TOS
         PSH   A
         JSR       MULT          **10 * DECNUM on TOS
         LDA   A   0, X          **get @LINE CHAR
         SUB   A   #HEX          **subtract $30
         PSH   A                 **@LINE — HEX on TOS
         PUL   A
         PUL   B
         ABA                     **10 * DECNUM + (@LINE — HEX)
         STA   A   DECNUM        **DECNUM:=
*
         INX                     **LINE:= LINE + 1
*
         BRA       WHILE         **END LOOP
         LDA   A   DECNUM
         RTS
end BLUE₂
```

This routine may be optimized even further by the reader, but its meaning will be obscured. Indeed, the routine may require additional safeguards. For example, there are no precautions against overflow. If the string of ASCII characters exceeds three digits, the value will not fit into an 8-bit DECNUM. This may very well occur, since three digit numbers like 523 are likely.

In addition, the BINARY routine is extendable to include the conversion of negative numbers. This is done by testing for a leading minus sign in the ASCII string of characters.

The next software wheel does the opposite of BINARY. The ASCII routine converts a single byte, decimal-equivalent binary number into an ASCII string. The number is initially taken from the stack, converted, and output to the location specified by the index register.

BLUE$_0$: ASCII
1. Convert an 8-bit byte into a signed, 3-digit ASCII string at location @LINE.
2. Method: Repeatedly divide the quotient by 10, producing a new quotient and remainder.
   (a) Push the remainder onto the stack;
   (b) use the quotient for subsequent divides;
   (c) stop when the quotient reaches zero.
3. Repeatedly pull the remainders from the stack and store them in an ASCII string.
4. Remember to test for the sign of the byte, and if necessary, push a minus sign onto the stack.
5. Also remember that repeated division by 10 produces the decimal digits from least-significant to most-significant digits. The stack reverses this order, thereby producing the correct order of output.

end BLUE$_0$

The method proposed is the inverse of the "shift-and-add" algorithm. Suppose we convert the binary version of 538 using the suggestion, above. The division by ten produces the following remainders and quotients:

Division	Quotient	Remainder
538/10	53	8
53/10	5	3
5/10	0	5

Now, notice the sequence of remainders produced by the three divisions. The digits have been produced in reverse order: 8, 3, and 5. We can reverse them by pushing them onto the stack, then pulling them in the order 5, 3, and 8.

Finally, the results may be stored as ASCII strings by addition of the zone bits; for example, $30. These functions and others are performed by the speedcode version that follows.

```
BLUE₁: Speedcode for ASCII
     ASCII: procedure (BYTE: tosbyte, @LINE: accx);
            var     I : byte;
            var QUOT : byte;
            var    REM : byte;
            const HEX : byte = $30;
            ;
            I:= 0
            if (BYTE < 0) then
                          MINUS: PUSH:= —;
                                 BYTE:= COMP (BYTE);
                                 I:= I + 1;
                      end if;
            QUOT:= BYTE;
            while (QUOT > 0) loop;
                QUOT:= QUOT/10, REM;
                PUSH:= REM;
                I:= I + 1;
```

```
        end loop;
        ;
        while (I > 0) loop
            @LINE:= PULL + HEX;
            LINE:= LINE + 1;
            I:= I — 1;
        end loop;
        ;
        return
    end ASCII
end BLUE₁
```

The PUSH, PULL, and COMP operations in the speedcode version, above, perform stack PUSH, stack PULL, and two's complement arithmetic, respectively. The division by ten produces a quotient and remainder as illustrated in earlier chapters. Consider the speedcode statement

```
QUOT:= QUOT/10, REM;
```

The double-valued result is to store the quotient of (QUOT/10) back into variable QUOT, and simultaneously store the remainder of (QUOT/10) into variable REM. The comma separates these two variables. Perhaps an alternate way to express this would have been to write:

```
QUOT, REM:= QUOT/10;
```

Either form must end up producing code similar to this 6800 kludgecode.

```
LDA   A   QUOT
PSH   A
LDA   A   #10
PSH   A
JSR       DIV        QUOT/10
PUL   A
STA   A   QUOT       QUOT:=
PUL   A
STA   A   REM        REM:=
```

The remaining lines of kludgecode are obtained directly from the speedcode.

The ASCII string obtained from an input routine like INBYTE may contain both numeric and alphabetical data. A convenient routine to include as another spoke in the software wheel is the TEST module. The TEST program returns a flag indicating whether a character is a number (+1) or an alphabetic (—1). Its specification is given below.

```
BLUE₀: TEST
    1. Set ACCB to:
        (+1) if ACCA contains a numeric character
        (—1) if ACCA contains a non-numeric character
```

```
            2. Return the flag in ACCB
end BLUE₀
```

The speedcode for such a routine is here given in **BLUE₁** form.

```
BLUE₁: Speedcode for TEST
       TEST: procedure (CHAR : acca)
                   var          FLAG : byte;
                   var          BCD  : byte;
                   ;
                   FLAG:= —1;
                   BCD:= CHAR—$30
                   if (BCD ≤ 9) then
                               MAYBE:
                               if BED ≥ 0 then
                                           YES: FLAG:= 1
                               end if;
                   end if;
                   return (FLAG : accb);
       end TEST
end BLUE₁
```

The kludgecode for this routine is easily implemented for the 8080 or 6800 architecture. In the 8080 we use registers A and B, and in the 6800 we use ACCA and ACCB.

Racing Wheels

Every software development project is accelerated by having a collection of modules that provide the basic building blocks for large systems. These modules usually take the form of arithmetic functions, I/O functions, and search/sort functions. Indeed, many of the tools have been developed for the reader in previous chapters.

In this section we illustrate the development of a small system that uses the software wheels typically needed in any software system. The problem to be solved by the illustrated example is called the Pocket Calculator problem. Suppose we define a Pocket Calculator as a machine that accepts alternate numbers and operators as input. When the last number is entered and = is entered, the calculator must perform the operations and print the answer.

```
BLUE₀: Pocket Calculator
       1. Compare the formula: #op#op . . . #op#=.
       2. Input the string above and store it internally as a BCD number string
          with alternate special characters (the operators +, —, *, /).
       3. Use BCD arithmetic to compute the result and display it as a BCD
          answer.
       4. Maintain a table that tells what to do after each character is input.
       5. Maintain a stack for storage of intermediate results.
       6. Terminate the input string with a carriage return, CR.
end BLUE₀
```

The Pocket Calculator problem is an opportunity to illustrate many of the ideas in this book. We can imagine the input to appear as the following example.

$$10*5-3/2 = CR$$

This input is put into postfix notation by a *table-driven* routine.

$$10 \quad 5 \quad * \quad 3 \quad 2 \quad / \quad - \quad =$$

The table that drives the input-to-reverse notation is given in Fig. 6.1. The columns of this table are labeled with the acceptable input characters and the rows of the table are labeled with the possible TOS characters. An input character is matched with a column label, and the top of stack character matched with the row label. The intersection entry gives a rule for converting the input to postfix notation. The conversion to postfix notation is done along with the following actions:

    i. read a character,
    ii. look-up rule in the table,
    iii. perform the rule given in the table,
    iv. repeat.

An example will illustrate the operation of the table in Fig. 6.1 and the input routine. Suppose the input string is given as follows.

$$10/3 + 5*8 = CR$$

Actions: output 10; push / on TOS; output 3
Result : +5*8 = CR
Stack : /
Output: 10 3

The next sequence of actions results in reducing the input string and increasing the output as a postfix notation result.

Actions: pop /, then push +; output 5; push *
Result : 8 = CR
Stack : + *
Output: 10 3 / 5

The "pop /" rule says to pull the TOS frame and write it out. The "push +" operation places the + symbol on the TOS. The "push *" rule also places * on the TOS. Finally, the "=" is reached and we get the postfix notation.

Actions: output 8; pop *
Result : CR
Stack :
Output: 10 3 / 5 8 * +

The resultant output string is ready to be processed into a final answer. We can do this by simply reading the reversed (postfix notation) string from left to right. Whenever an operator is encountered, we perform the operation. Whenever a constant is encountered we push it onto the TOS. Thus, we are back to the speedcode streamlining method, only this time the machine is programmed to do the streamlining for us.

```
TABLE: procedure (@OUTPUT: accx);
        var    CHAR : byte
        const  CR    : byte = #$OD;
        ;
        push:= '    ' : (initialize the stack)
        loop;
                CHAR:= INBYTE
                while  (CHAR ⩾ 0 and
                        CHAR ⩽ 9      ) loop;
                        CHAR:= CHAR — 0; (convert to BCD)
                        @OUTPUT:= CHAR;
                        OUTPUT:= OUTPUT + 1;
                        CHAR:= INBYTE ; (get next CHAR)
                        end loop;
        ;
        case   CHAR  of;
        "+"    : PLUS    (CHAR: acca);
        "—"    : MINUS   (CHAR: acca);
        "*"    : TIMES   (CHAR: acca);
        "/"    : DIVIDE  (CHAR: acca);
        "="    : COMP    (CHAR: acca);
        end case;
        end loop when (CHAR = CR);
        return
end TABLE
```

The TABLE routine performs an "output" operation if the input is a digit, and calls the appropriate processing routine to complete the reverse notation if the input is not a digit. These routines perform the rule indicated in Table 6.1. For example, the PLUS, MINUS, TIMES, and DIVIDE routines do the following. The COMP routine calls other modules which in turn process the reverse output string.

```
PLUS: procedure (CHAR: acca);
        var TOS : byte;
        ; (examine the TOS element)
        TOS:= pull; push:= TOS;
        case TOS of;
        "    "  :  "+"  :  push:= CHAR;
        " — "  :  "*"  :  "/"  :  @OUTPUT:= pull;
                                  OUTPUT:= OUTPUT + 1;
                                  push:= CHAR;
        end case;
        return;
end PLUS;
MINUS: procedure (CHAR : acca)
```

Table 6.1 Postfix rule for Pocket Calculator.

What is on TOS	"digit"	+ or −	* or /	=
"space"	output	push	push	error
+	output	push	push	pop†
−	output	pop; push	push	pop†
*	output	pop; push	pop; push	pop†
/	output	pop; push	pop; push	pop†

†pop Pull from the stack until it is empty.

```
              PLUS (CHAR : ACCA);
          return;
      end MINUS;
      TIMES: procedure (CHAR : acca)
             var  TOS : byte;
             TOS:= pull;
             push:= TOS;
             case  TOS  of;
             " " : "+" : "−"  :  push:= CHAR;
             "*"  : "/"  :     @OUTPUT:= pull;
                               OUTPUT:= OUTPUT + 1;
                               push:= CHAR;
             end case;
             return;
      end TIMES;
      DIVIDE: procedure (CHAR : acca);
             TIMES (CHAR : acca);
             return;
      end DIVIDE
```

The remaining modules for the Pocket Calculator system must perform BCD arithmetic on numbers of arbitrary length. This can be done in the 6800 and 8080 processors by issuing a DAA instruction after every ADD and SUB instruction. The DAA instruction "corrects" the binary arithmetic by adjusting it to force a BCD result in the accumulator. Thus, if every ADD and SUB is followed by a DAA operation, the results will always remain in BCD (assuming they started in BCD).

A final example of racing wheels is given in speedcode form. The high speed sorting module QUICK is a program that accepts an array of N bytes and sorts them into ascending order. The QUICK algorithm is fast, but somewhat difficult to understand. It operates as shown by the following example.

Suppose we order the list

$$8 \quad 3 \quad 5 \quad 7 \quad 2 \quad 6 \quad e$$

into an ascending list of numbers. The QUICK method selects the middle element as a temporary, say element $(7/2)$ = element 3, and sets it aside as element T.

$$T = 5$$
$$J = N = 7$$
$$I = 1$$

Two pointers, I and J are set-up to begin scanning the unordered list. The lower one-half of the list is searched for an element greater than T, while the upper half of the list is searched for an element less than T.

$$T = 5$$
$$I = 1$$
$$J = 7$$

⑧   3   5   7   2   6   ③

These two values are exchanged and the search for a value less than T and a corresponding value greater than T continues by decreasing J and increasing I.

3   3   5   ⑦   ②   6   8
$$T = 5$$
$$I = 4$$
$$J = 5$$

These values are exchanged and the process repeats itself. Eventually the upper and lower scans meet each other and we must begin the second phase of QUICK.

3   3   5   2   ┊   7   6   8

lower   ┊   upper

Notice a very important feature of the two sublists. Every number in the lower sublist is less than or equal to T, and every element in the upper sublist is greater than T. Thus, with respect to T, the sublists are in their proper place in the (eventually) ordered list. The only thing remaining to be done is to order the lower sublist, then order the upper sublist. We can do this by splitting the sublists away from one another, and *recursively* apply the sort routine again to each sublist.

Recursion. A recursive subroutine is a subroutine that calls itself.

Thus, we can complete the QUICK module by passing the left half of the original list to it, then the right half, and then recursively processing the sublists until every sub-sublist is ordered.

QUICK [X (1 . . N)] = QUICK [X (1 . . M)] ; QUICK [X (M + 1 . . N)]

In the example above we can process the lower and upper sublists in a recursive manner.

QUICK [   ] = QUICK [3, 3, 5, 2] ; QUICK [7, 6, 8]

The recursion is done by pushing the values established during the calculation onto the stack and then calling the routine, itself. When a return is executed, the return address is taken from the stack along with the values as they were upon entry to the recursive subroutine. Hence the return must not only restore the return address, but it must also restore the values of variables used during an earlier execution of the same code.

An example of the restoration of values is given by the values of T, I, and J in the QUICK routine.

A fully operable QUICK sorting routine must also provide for boundary conditions that may arise. For example, it is usually too inefficient to apply recursion to lists of less than 12 elements. Therefore a straightforward selection sort is usually applied to short sublists.

Additionally, the QUICK sort routine must be able to cope with lists that are already in order! For example, suppose we give QUICK the ordered array

$$1 \quad 2 \quad 3 \quad 4 \quad 5 \quad 6 \quad 7$$

The QUICK routine would search for an element in the lower sublist that is greater than 3 while looking in the upper sublist for a number less than 3. The searches would fail to locate any such numbers until the 4 is reached. At the point where the lower search reaches the upper search we have still found no elements to exchange. The list is divided into a lower and upper portion, in the example above, but eventually we would end up with a sublist that is difficult to divide into two sublists, namely, the list containing one element.

This anomaly is usually overcome by an initial exchange with T. The first element of the list is put into the position occupied by element (N/2). Then the search begins with the second element of the list. When the middle point is reached, the middle element is copied back into the first position, and the value of T is written into the middle element's position. This "trick" is illustrated by the short sequence below.

Start	:	7	6	8	
Find T	:	7	⑥	8	T = 6
Copy	:	7 →	7	8	T = 6
Search from the second element	:	7 :	7	8	T = 6
Copy T back to first	:	6 :	7	8	
Divide list	:	(6)	(7	8)	

Clearly the QUICK routine is a sophisticated piece of software. An extensive blueprint streamlining process is necessary in order to produce the finished product. We present only a beginning specification of the solution.

```
Blueprint for QUICK
        QUICK [X(1 . . N)] =
            J:= N; I:= 1; T:= X(N/2);
            if (N ≤ 12) then
                        SHORT: SSORT (X(1 . . N));
                        return
            else;
                    while (true) loop;
                    if (I = J) then QUICK (X(1 . . I)); QUICK (X(I + 1 . . N));
                                    return;
                    else
                        if (X(I) > T) then
                                if (X(J) < T) then "exchange X(I)
                                                and X(J), and
                                                increment I"
                                else J:= J — 1;
                                end if;
                    else
                        if (X(J) < T) then "do nothing"
                                    else J:= J — 1;
                        end if
                    I:= I + 1;
                    end if;
                    end if;
                    end loop;
            end QUICK
    end BLUEPRINT
```

This specification is incomplete. Its completion is left to the reader as an exercise. Beware, however, the "trick" discussed earlier concerning the exchange between T and element one. It has not been incorporated in this specification. We left it out in order to simplify the explanation. Even so, the specification requires extensive study.

We return now to the subject of I/O. Most microprocessors are capable of more sophisticated I/O mechanisms than those derived in the preceding sections. Indeed, the widespread utilization of microprocessors in appliances and instrumentation depends on a form of I/O that allows the processor to overlap I/O with other processing. This form of overlap is accomplished by using the *interrupt structure* of the processor.

In and Out, In and Out

Most microprocessors incorporate a mechanism for handling *exceptions*. An exception is a hardware activated event that is synchronized by an *interrupt structure*. For example, the hardware activated events

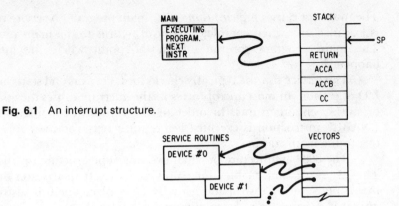

Fig. 6.1 An interrupt structure.

"overflow," "zero divide," and "input done" are performed by hardware circuits that alert the software through a signal called the "interrupt."

An interrupt routine can be thought of as a "hardware called subroutine." Whenever an exception occurs, the hardware automatically calls a *service routine* to take care of the interrupt. The service routine must be written by a programmer and its location given to the interrupt structure. This is where programming comes into the picture.

An *interrupt vector* is a location in memory containing the address of a service routine. Interrupt vectors often contain return addresses, status values, etc. But for our purposes, the interrupt vector is simply an address for the interrupt structure to use to call a service routine.

The interrupt vectors of the 8080 architecture, for example, reside in memory locations 0, 10_{16}, 20_{16}, . . ., 80_{16}. An RST (restart) instruction causes the 8080 to begin executing the instructions at one of these vectors. RST 1 begins execution at location 10, for instance. Typically, the first instruction executed at location 0, 10_{16} . . . is a JMP to the service routine.

The structure in Fig. 6.1 illustrates the relationship between interrupts and the "other" program executing between interrupts. The MAIN program executes as if no other process is active in the microprocessor. If and when an interrupt occurs, the location of a service routine is selected from the interrupt vector corresponding to the interrupt. The routine is executed and control returns to the main program. Note the return address is stacked as if a normal subroutine has been executed.

An exception is made to happen when an I/O routine is executed in *concurrent mode*. The routine typically separates the two phases discussed earlier. In the case of an input operation, the input is started and allowed to run concurrently with the main program. When all data has been transferred into the microprocessor memory, an interrupt occurs.

The interrupt causes *pre-emption* of the main program. A service routine is executed and when completed, control returns to the main program. The main program continues from the point where the interrupt happened.

The service routine typically checks for I/O errors and starts another I/O operation. In most microprocessors the interrupt causes the *disabling* of subsequent interrupts. In order to allow subsequent interrupts, an ENABLE instruction is executed before the service routine returns control to the main routine.

The 8080 architecture provides two interrupt structure instructions. The EI instruction enables interrupts and the DI instruction disables interrupts. The EI instruction actually takes place one full instruction *after* it is executed in order to allow a RET from the service routine.

The 6800 architecture provides for two kinds of interrupts. The NMI (nonmaskable interrupts) cannot be disabled. The MI (maskable interrupts) can be disabled using the SEI (set I) instruction. The CLI (clear I) instruction enables maskable interrupts. Thus, the correspondence between 8080 and 6800 interrupt instructions is given below.

8080	6800
DI	SEI
EI	CLI

Furthermore, the 6800 has two useful instructions called "wait," and "software interrupt." The WAI instruction causes the microprocessor to wait for an interrupt, while the SWI causes an interrupt. Note also that the 6800 registers are automatically stacked whenever an interrupt occurs. This means that a special return instruction is needed to unstack (restore) the register before leaving the service routine. The RTI (return from interrupt) instruction accomplishes the restore as well as return.

There are four interrupt vectors in the 6800. The two system vectors (one for NMI and the other for MI), and a user vector (works with SWI) are located in the highest location of memory. The system-wide RESET interrupt vector is in the last two bytes, followed by the other three.

Address	Type
FFFE	RESET
FFFC	NMI
FFFA	SWI
FFF8	MI

Thus, we would establish a maskable interrupt software system as follows in the 6800.

```
                ORG     $FFF8       vector location
MIVEC           FDB     $4000       MI service
SWIVEC          FDB     $5000       SWI service
NMIVEC          FDB     $6000       NMI service
RSTVEC          FDB     $7000       RESTART routine
                ORG     $4000
SERVICE         ____
                ____
                ____
                RTI
                ORG     $5000
SWIR            ____
                ____
                ____
                RTI
                ORG     $6000
MNIR            ____
                ____
                ____
                etc.
```

These routines are executed when the appropriate interrupt occurs. Suppose we design a concurrent I/O routine that processes an input stream at the "same time" as another program is running. The blueprints for such a routine must include both set-up and interrupt servicing routines.

BLUE$_0$: Concurrent I/O
1. Store characters in a buffer area in memory as they are (concurrently) input.
2. Halt the input when the buffer becomes full, or else a CR is input.
3. Use a table to keep track of the concurrent input process.
end BLUE$_0$

The startup routine is used to initialize flags, counters, and the buffer index. It must be executed before any interrupts are allowed to occur. Therefore, we surround the startup code with disabling–enabling instructions.

```
STARTUP : procedure ( );
            var     FLAGIN : byte;
            var     INDEX  : byte;
            var     COUNT  : byte;
            const   BUF     : word = $5500;
                    disable; FLAGIN:= $80;
                             INDEX:= #BUF — 1;
                             COUNT:= 64;
                    enable;
            return
end STARTUP
```

The kludgecode for this routine would be located anywhere in memory, and resemble the 6800 version.

```
STARTUP    SEI                        **disable
           LDA   A   #$80
           STA   A   FLAGIN           **FLAGIN:= $80.
           LDX       #BUF — 1
           STX       INDEX            **set up index register
           LDA   A   #64
           STA   A   COUNT            **COUNT:= 64
           CLI                        **enable
           RTS
FLAGIN     RMB       1
INDEX      RMB       2
COUNT      RMB       1
BUF        EQU       $5500
           END
```

The interrupt routine must be located in a position of memory that is known to the SWIVEC, say. Thus, the interrupt procedure is placed in location $5000.

```
INDATA : interrupt procedure (@INDEX: accx) = $5000;
         disable;
         if (FLAGIN = $80) then
                       READ: INDEX:= INDEX + 1;
                             @INDEX:= INBYTE;
                             COUNT:= COUNT — 1;
             if (COUNT = 0 or
             @INDEX = CR) then
                           DONE: FLAGIN:= 0;
             end if;
           end if;
           enable;
           return;
end INDATA
```

The 6800 kludgecode for this service routine is located at $5000 as suggested by the SWI vector value.

```
           ORG       $FFFA
SWIVEC     FDB       $5000
           ORG       $5000
INDATA     SEI                        **disable
           TST       FLAGIN           **FLAGIN negative?
           BEQ       ENDIF2           **no
*   then clause
           INX                        **INDEX:= INDEX + 1
           JSR       INBYTE           **@INDEX:= INBYTE
           STA   A   0, X             **@INDEX:=
           DEC       COUNT            **COUNT:= COUNT — 1
*   secard if
           LDA   A   COUNT
           CMP   A   #0
```

```
              BNE      ENDIF1        **COUNT = 0?
              LDA   A  0, X          **get byte @INDEX
              CMP   A  #CR
              BNE      ENDIF1        **is it a CR?
DONE          CLR      FLAGIN        **FLAGIN 1 + 0
ENDIF1
ENDIF2        CLI                    **enable interrupts
              RTI                    **return from interrupt
              END
```

We can make this problem even more interesting by imagining a second interrupt routine that processes the input data, concurrently. Suppose, for example, an OUTDATA routine running from the maskable interrupt vector at location $4000 is used to output the line of characters to a printer. The printer runs asynchronously in parallel with the other routines.

```
OUTDATA : interrupt procedure (@OUTEX: accx) = $4000
          disable;
          if (FLAGIN = $00) then;
                        WRITE: OUTEX:= OUTEX + 1;
                               OUTCHAR (@OUTEX: accx);
                               NO:= NO — 1;
                        if (NO = 0 OR
                           @OUTEX = CR) then;
                           FLIP: FLAGIN:= $80;
                        end if;
          end if;
          enable;
          return
end OUTDATA
```

This routine is quite similar to the INDATA routine. Note, however, that the output is held up until the "flagin" value is cleared. This means that an entire line is input before any output characters begin to be processed through the printer.

A truly parallel (asynchronously serial) *co-routine* pair would overlap their execution without regard to the value of FLAGIN. The only danger in doing this occurs if the "reader" falls behind the "writer," or the "reader" overwrites the buffer before it is emptied by the "writer."

We can guarantee the security of the buffer of data by counting the number of characters that remain to be output by OUTCHAR. Whenever the count goes to zero, we must delay the OUTDATA service routine to allow INDATA to catch up.

The INDATA routine will not be allowed to overrun the buffer (by attempting to fill it a second, third, etc. time), because of FLAGIN. Thus, we need only keep track of the number of characters still waiting to be written out by the WRITE section of OUTDATA.

If the number of characters input to the buffer by INDATA is greater than the number of characters output by OUTDATA, then the OUTDATA routine is allowed to continue.

$$\text{Number input} = 64 - COUNT$$
$$\text{Number output} = 64 - NO$$

$$64 - COUNT > 64 - NO$$

$$COUNT \leqslant NO$$

Hence, we must insert a TEST in the OUTDATA routine.

```
TEST: if (COUNT ≤ NO) then
                    WRITE:
              else
                    WAIT; goto TEST;
      end if
```

This piece of code will allow the OUTDATA routine to continue (write) if the data is available. Otherwise, the WAIT statement is executed (this causes a WAI instruction to be produced in the 6800). When the INDATA routine executes, the WAIT is cleared and the OUTDATA routine can test the counts once again.

The test is used in OUTDATA in place of the comparison for FLAGIN. The two co-routines can now overlap their execution between input and output.

The INDATA/OUTDATA problem we have just described is a very common problem in nearly all computers with an interrupt structure. The COUNT and NO comparison produces a *true* or *false* result. This flag is called a *semaphore*, and the problem just described is called the *semaphore problem*.

A semaphore is used to control access to shared data. In the INDATA/OUTDATA example, the buffer and its corresponding counters and pointers are shared by both co-routines. Whenever we write a program that shares data in this fashion we call the programs a *critical section of code*.

This chapter completes the study of programming as a methodology. In the next few chapters we investigate the underlying structure of software tools, for example, the assembler and the speedcode language.

7
Kludgecode at the
Speed of Light

I once knew a programmer,
whose name was Henry the Third.

His bugs were known to be slight,
but once they propagated
at the speed of light!

And now, we call him Henry the Nerd.

*　　*　　*

The Heart of the Assembler

One of the most valuable tools used throughout this book is a program called the assembler. An assembler is simply a program, and as such is subject to the same kind of analysis as any other program. Indeed, many of the software wheels reinvented in this text are used by assembler designers to implement new assemblers.

It is not necessary to develop an assembler in order to program microprocessors, yet an understanding of the design of an assembler will make better programmers. In the following sections we develop a cursory model for symbolic assembly.

Assembly. The process of translating symbolic machine language into binary machine language.

Microprocessors employ a variety of assembly languages. Each language reflects the architecture of the microprocessor, so there can be no universal assembly language. The differences among assemblers is not great, however, and so an understanding of one assembler is usually sufficient to grasp how all assemblers work.

It is the purpose of any assembler to convert the symbolic addresses (labels) and the symbolic op-codes (mnemonics) into executable binary patterns. This is done with the aid of a *symbol table*.

Mnemonic	Hex value	Addressing mode increment				Other info
		IMM	DIR	IND	EXT	
ADDA	8B	00	10	20	30	
ADDB	CB	00	10	20	30	
ANDA	84	00	10	20	30	
ANDB	C4	00	10	20	30	
ABA	1B	—	—	—	—	
ADCA	89	00	10	20	30	
ADCB	C9	00	10	20	30	
ASLA	48	—	—	—	—	
ASLB	58	—	—	—	—	
ASLM	68	—	—	00	10	
WAI	3E	—	—	—	—	

IMM: immediate
DIR: direct
IND: indexed
EXT: extended direct

Fig. 7.1 Mnemonic table for the 6800.

Symbol Table. A table containing the labels of a given program along with the values (addresses) of the labels.

The symbol table is constructed by reading the program. Each label is read and its corresponding location beyond the beginning of the program is entered next to the label in the symbol table. This is called *pass one* of the assembly process.

A second table is held within the assembler. This is the *mnemonic table*, or table containing all symbolic instructions along with their binary-valued equivalents. The mnemonic table is used to calculate the values of labels in pass one and, more importantly, to replace the mnemonics used by a programmer with the executable binary code. Thus, a second pass over the program is required in order to generate proper instructions. The actual executable machine code is produced by *pass two* of the assembler.

Figure 7.1 illustrates part of the mnemonic table for the Motorola 6800 symbolic assembly language. Note the various addressing modes in the figure. Each op-code produced by pass two is the sum of the hex value plus the addressing mode value.

The mnemonic table does not change and grow during assembly like the symbol table. It is usually built into the assembler and merely referenced during pass two. In some machines, the mnemonic table contains other information; the length of the instruction, for example.

The heart of an assembler is its symbol table. Fig. 7.2 gives a part of a symbol table created during pass one. The symbol table may contain additional information, such as the type of label (subprocedure name, entry point, variable, constant, etc.).

It is important to remember that the symbol table is constructed as pass one reads the assembler language statements. Each label is defined by inserting the value (address) of the label next to its name.

Since symbol tables are tables that grow, they may overflow occasionally. In addition, the symbols stored there must be unique. If they are not unique, the symbol table will notify the programmer that duplicate labels were found in the program.

Pass One

Suppose we illustrate the first pass over the source code below. This pass will build a symbol table for use by the second pass. The program does nothing of value, but it serves a useful purpose by demonstrating what happens to various symbols when fed to the assembler program.

```
          ORG     $1000
STACK     RMB     1
STATUS    EQU     $F000
VARI      FCB     $5
ENTRY     LDA   A VARI
LOOP2     STA   A SAVE
          LDS     #STACK
          LDA   A STATUS
          ROR   A
          BVC     LOOP2
          LDA   A STATUS + 1
          RTS
SAVE      FCB     #0
          END
```

After pass one the symbol table contains the names and values of all labels found in the program.

Fig. 7.2 A symbol table from pass one.

Label	Value	Other
WLOOP	$5020	–
MULT	$3F02	–
AGAIN	$3F0I	–
Y	$4I00	–
R	$4I02	–
S	$4I03	–
⋮	⋮	⋮

Label	Value
STACK	1000
STATUS	F000
VARI	1001
ENTRY	1002
LOOP2	1005
SAVE	1014

We might imagine the source program as being reduced to an intermediate form as shown below.

```
1000   ORG     $1000
1000   RMB     1
1001   FCB     #5
1002   LDA   A VARI
1005   STA   A SAVE
       LDS     #STACK
       LDA   A STATUS
       ROR   A
       BVC     LOOP2
       LDA   A STATUS + 1
       RTS
1014   FCB     #0
       END
```

This version of the program probably would *not* be produced by a "smart" assembler. The reason is that several of the instructions (LDA and STA) may take advantage of direct or extended addressing. The extended addressing mode uses one more byte of memory than the direct mode. We have assumed an extended mode in this hypothetical example.

Pass Two

The second pass produces binary (executable) code from the mnemonic table. Pass two uses the values stored in the symbol table to compute the address field of instructions accessing main memory. We will use extended addressing throughout the following example. The branch instructions take advantage of an additional addressing mode called PC-relative. In this mode, the second byte of the branch instruction is added to the PC (program counter) to arrive at an effective (actual) address.

Pass two produces the correspondence shown below. The resultant code is executable.

Location	Mnemonic (before)			Binary (hex)	
1000	RMB		1	?	
1001	FCB		#5	05	
1002	LDA	A	$1001	B6	1001
1005	STA	A	$1014	87	1014
1008	LDS		#$1000	BE	1000
100B	LDA	A	$F000	B6	F000
100E	ROR	A		46	
100F	BVC		$1005-$1010	28	F5
1010	LDA	A	$F000 + 1	B6	F001
1013	RTS			39	
1014	FCB		#0		

The correspondence between "before and after" is straightforward in every statement above except the branch statement. In the BVC statement, the PC-relative address of the branch is obtained as an 8-bit, two's complement displacement from the next instruction following the BVC instruction. Therefore, we perform the hexadecimal operation as follows:

$$\begin{array}{r} 1005 \\ - \ 1010 \\ \hline \text{FFF5} \end{array}$$

This result is obtained by borrowing a carry from the most significant bit position beyond the four hexadecimal digits shown above.

Since FFF5 will not fit into a single byte of memory, only F5 is generated and stored. When the instruction is executed, the PC-relative address is computed by *sign extension*. That is, the leading (sign) bit of the 8-bit byte is replicated in the most significant 8-bits of a 16-bit word. Thus, F5 is extended into the original FFF5.

During execution of the BVC instruction the branch address will be either 1010 (no branch) or else,

$$\begin{array}{r} 1010 \\ + \ \text{FFF5} \\ \hline 1 \leftarrow \quad 1005 \end{array}$$

The carry-out is discarded, and the value 1005 used as the next instruction address. Thus, the microprocessor is able to branch forward 7F bytes or backward $(-7F + 1) = FF$ bytes.

An assembler is frequently given the responsibility of producing *relocatable object code*. Such code is easily moved to any place in main memory. In the example above we did not produce relocatable code. For example, the following statements produce nonrelocatable code in the 6800.

```
LDA   A   VARI
STA   A   SAVE
```

If we move the object code for this program to another place in memory the values of VARI and SAVE also change. For example, if we move the program to $2000, then these instructions must also be modified to show the change in VARI and SAVE.

Before		After	
B6	1001	B6	2001
B7	1014	B7	2014

A relocatable assembler produces an intermediate form consisting of the machine code with tags indicating that an instruction must be relocated. For example, let R be the relocate tag, then the output of pass two would appear as shown below.

```
00
05
B6       1001R
B7       1014R
8E       1000
B6       F000
46
28       F5
B6       F001
39
00
```

This intermediate form is loaded by a *relocating loader* that computes an offset value for each tagged op-code. The offset is added to the instruction before the instruction is stored in memory.

A *linking loader* takes many subprocedures and relocates them in memory, then computes the offset needed to generate correct addresses for all JSR (jump subroutine) calls.

Pass two is complete when all intermediate code and the necessary tables for loaders have been produced.

8
Speedcode at the Speed of Light

Word spread rapidly through the Empire on that sun-softened spring morning of 2019 A.D. Every newsviewer from Venus to the Rings of Saturn broadcast his picture in 3D and living color. His voice was heard from talkshows in Marsport, selling spacehockey puks in Luna, and giving testimonials for terramobiles in New Chicago. Carboli Gabolis was the most famous human in the solar system within the span of a single day following announcement of his revolutionary computer.

Until Gabolis invented the CG6000 computer, every computer before was limited by the speed of light. That is, they were able to compute only as fast as the speed of light would allow. This meant that very sophisticated computations sometimes required hours of computer time. The era of "slow" computers was over, however, because Gabolis and his assistant Flandrena, had stumbled onto a computer that was faster than the speed of light!

The only obstacle to the revolutionary CG6000 was its user interface. It was difficult to use a computer so fast that it printed an answer before the question was asked.

*   *   *

Speedcode is a proven blueprint language for reducing the time and cost of programming a microcomputer. Indeed, if it were possible to automatically translate from speedcode to kludgecode, then microcomputer programming would never need to be concerned with the low level details of kludgecode. In fact, this is the case.

Kludgecode is unnecessary.

A number of techniques for translating from speedcode languages into kludgecode languages are well known. In this chapter we begin the study of these techniques and show the reader how to automate the streamlining process so a machine can do it, instead.

There are additional benefits to learning the secrets of automatic streamlining:

  i. to understand how computers work;
 ii. to generalize on what we have learned so far;
iii. to understand why new microprocessor architectures are being built the way they are, instead of the way they have been in the past.

Once programmers are liberated from the drudgery of kludgecode, the cost of software begins to level-off. Each speedcode statement is worth several kludgecode statements. Thus, speedcode is a software lever; it gives each programmer a mechanical advantage. Higher rates of productivity result, and most importantly, the low level detail of kludgecode is forgotten.

In the subsequent chapters we look into the metasystem tools for describing languages. These tools provide a general method of automating nearly any kind of speedcode. Next, we develop useful algorithms for implementing automatic compiling systems. And finally, the impact of software development tools (high level languages) is studied in the final chapter.

Thanks to BNF

The speedcode blueprint used to streamline microprocessor programs is actually a high level language. The method of streamlining to kludgecode is called *hand compiling*. That is, the programmer translates a single speedcode statement into one or more kludgecode statements, manually.

It is possible to write another program called a *compiler* that translates each speedcode statement into one or more kludgecode statements, automatically. Indeed, many microprocessor development systems supply such compiler programs for the express purpose of automating translation. Many of these compilers are sophisticated enough to convert each statement of speedcode into one or more flashcode (optimized) statements, directly. Therefore, some compilers are capable of producing better microprocessor programs than humans.

The purpose of this chapter is to show how to design and implement a compiler for high level languages like speedcode. Knowledge of compiling is useful in understanding one of the most important tools in software engineering. In the process of describing how a compiler works, we can also appreciate many ideas underlying computer science and software development.

One of the most useful ideas developed in the early 1960s by John Backus and Peter Naur was the special notation called Backus–Naur Form,

BNF. This notation is actually a simple language for defining programming languages. BNF is a *metalanguage*, because it describes other languages.

Actually, BNF was invented to describe only a part of a programming language. The *syntax* of a language is the collection of rules for producing grammatically correct sentences in a given language. The *semantics* of a language is the collection of rules for explaining the meaning of correct sentences in a given language. BNF is used to define the syntax of a language. The semantics of a language is more difficult to describe in general terms, so we will use kludgecode to define the semantics of each speedcode statement.

Thanks to BNF we can unambiguously define the grammar of a programming language. For example, suppose we want to define the grammar of speedcode assignment statements. What rules govern the following (correct?) statement?

$$X:= (S + 2)/B;$$

First, we note there are several "objects" in the speedcode language. The assignment statement has two kinds of objects: (1) names of variables, and (2) operator symbols. We can define the grammar of the simple assignment statement merely by defining the relationship between variables and operators. These relationships are called *production rules*, or simply, productions.

The variable and operator objects are actually made up of alphabetic and special symbols. These are called *terminal* objects because we cannot reduce them to any more primitive objects. A "terminal" is usually any character that can be found on a keyboard.

We use productions to build *non-terminal* objects from terminals. Thus, to construct a variable name in speedcode we combine one or more letters into a name. The letters are terminal symbols while the resulting name is a non-terminal. We can think of a non-terminal as being a word in normal English grammar. Furthermore, like English grammar, every "word" in speedcode belongs to a "part-of-speech." Thus, a name used as a variable belongs to a part-of-speech called "variable."

BNF is used to express the grammar of a programming language by defining how to combine terminals and non-terminals to form sentences. In BNF, a non-terminal is enclosed in "less-than" and "greater-than" metasymbols to set them apart from terminals. Thus, a variable is defined in terms of letters and/or numerals.

1. <variable>   ::=   <simple variable>
                         ::=   <subscripted variable>
2. <simple variable>   ::=   <letter>
                         ::=   <letter>   <alphameric>

3. <alphameric>   ::= <letter> <alphameric>
                          ::= <numeral> <alphameric>
                          ::= <letter>
                          ::= <digit>

4. <letter>   ::= A
                          ::= B
                          ::= C
                          ::= D
                          .
                          .
                          .
                          ::= Z

5. <numeral>   ::= 0
                          ::= 1
                          .
                          .
                          ::= 9

Notice how the "is defined as" symbol ::= is used to write a production in the form of an LHS (left-hand-side) and an RHS (right-hand-side). The LHS always consists of a single non-terminal while the RHS consists of one or more terminal and/or non-terminals. In addition, an RHS may be made up of one or more lines. The RHS can express optional forms, so if a variable is defined as either a simple variable or a subscripted variable, then two lines appear in the RHS. A simple variable is defined in turn as either a single letter or a letter followed by an alphameric.

The BNF production for defining an alphameric is "right-recursive" because it shows an RHS containing an alphameric, itself. Thus, BNF productions may be defined in terms of themselves. The production could also have been written in "left-recursive" form as follows:

    <alphameric> ::= <alphameric> <letter>
                 ::= <alphameric> <numeral>

Furthermore, we could have used both "right-recursive" and "left-recursive" forms by alternating the RHS.

    <alphameric> ::= <alphameric> <letter>
                 ::= <numeral>   <alphameric>

This form is often confusing to a compiler, and should be avoided. We can use the recursion to produce strings of arbitrary length, however. Production three, above, will produce a single letter, or a single letter followed by a single numeral, or two letters, or three alphameric characters, etc. Consider the following derivation obtained by repeated substitution into production three.

$$
\begin{aligned}
\text{<alphameric>} &\;::=\; \text{<letter> <alphameric>}\\
&\;::=\; \text{a <alphameric>}\\
&\;::=\; \text{a <letter> <alphameric>}\\
&\;::=\; \text{am <alphameric>}\\
&\;::=\; \text{am5 <alphameric>}\\
&\;::=\; \text{am5 <letter>}\\
&\;::=\; \text{am5z}
\end{aligned}
$$

We say "am5z" is *derived* from "alphameric" when we obtain the name by repeated application of the alphameric production.

A shorthand version of recursion can be used to clarify BNF statements. An * is often used to show repetition. Thus, we could define a string of letters (of arbitrary length), as follows.

<letter>*

This notation may be used to express the grammar of a simple variable.

$$
\begin{aligned}
\text{<simple variable>} &\;::=\; \text{<letter>}\\
&\;::=\; \text{<alphameric>*}
\end{aligned}
$$

Other abbreviations are used to clarify and simplify BNF, but the original BNF has withstood the test of time. Because of its simplicity, BNF will probably remain the best way to describe the grammar of a programming language. We demonstrate its simplicity and power by defining the grammar of a simple Speedcode expression. The "expression" is used in assignment statements, predicates, and parameter lists.

```
if (Y = (S + 3) *B) then
                GO: M:= (Y + B)/2;
                else
                NOGO: M:= —M;
end if
```

We want to develop a collection of productions in BNF that defines the predicates, assignments, and **if-then-else** clauses, above. The total description of speedcode is prepared in a similar manner. The result is a grammatical definition of an entire language (this takes about 300–400 productions).

The grammar of an expression must serve multiple purposes: predicates, assignments, etc. Thus, we define each line of an RHS for each of the intended purposes.

$$
\begin{aligned}
1.\;\; \text{<expression>} &\;::=\; \text{<logical factor>}\\
&\;::=\; \text{<expression> } \mathbf{or} \text{ <logical factor>}
\end{aligned}
$$

The non-terminal "expression" is defined in "left-recursion" form as either another non-terminal called "logical factor," or else a compound string consisting of a subexpression in a logical "OR" expression. The "OR" is a terminal object defined as the "OR" operator.

2. <logical factor>   ::=   <logical secondary>
                     ::=   <logical factor> **and** <logical secondary>

Again, "logical factor" is defined in "left-recursive" form involving the "AND" operator. Thus, we have defined the non-terminal "expression" as either the right-hand-side of an assignment statement, or as part of a predicate.

$$:= Y + 2;$$
$$(Y \text{ and } T)$$

We need to define the "logical secondary," next.

3. <logical secondary>   ::=   <logical primary>
                        ::=   **not** <logical primary>

This production gives Speedcode the power of negation. For example,

$$(\textbf{not } Y \text{ and } Z)$$

can be evaluated in a predicate. But what is the grammar of a "logical primary"?

4. <logical primary>   ::=   <sum>
                       ::=   <sum> > <sum>
                       ::=   <sum>>= <sum>
                       ::=   <sum> <><sum>
                       ::=   <sum> <= <sum>
                       ::=   <sum> < <sum>
                       ::=   <sum> = <sum>

The Boolean operators for comparison in a predicate are defined by production four. Next we define the four arithmetic operations.

5. <sum>   ::=   <term>
            ::=   <sum> + <term>
            ::=   <sum> — <term>
            ::=   —<term>
            ::=   +<term>

At this point in developing the grammar, we have defined the simple expressions of predicates and arithmetic operations.

$$Y + 5$$
$$Y > 5$$
$$\textbf{not } Y + 0$$
$$-Y + 5$$

We need more structure to express complex terms.

6.   <term>   ::=   <factor>
              ::=   <term> * <factor>
              ::=   <term> / <factor>

This gives speedcode the power of multiplication and division. The non-terminal "factor" gives the grammar the power of exponentiation.

7.   <factor>   ::=   <primary>
              ::=   <factor>   ** <primary>

A "primary" is either a variable or a constant. In a more extensive definition, we would include function names (subprocedures) as another possible value of a "primary." For brevity, we omit the subprocedure reference.

8.   <primary>   ::=   <variable>
              ::=   <constant>

Finally we define "variable" as before.

9.   <variable>   ::=   <simple variable>
              ::=   <subscripted variable>

10.   <subscripted variable>   ::=   <simple variable>(<expression>)
                                ::=   <simple variable> (expression>,
                                        <expression>)

Thus, "subscripted variables" can be one-, or two-dimensional only.

We could continue to develop the entire speedcode language in this manner. For example, the **if-then-else, while, var,** and **procedure** statements can be defined in BNF.

11. <if stmt> ::= **if** (<expression>) **then**
<label>
<then clause>
else
<label>
<else clause>
end if

12. <while> ::= **while** (<expression>) **loop**
<while body>
end loop

The BNF description may appear to be time-consuming and of more theoretical interest than practical value. It is extremely practical, however, when combined with a *compiler system*. A compiler system accepts BNF as input along with a speedcode program. The speedcode program is translated into kludgecode by the compiler system under the guidance of the BNF productions. Therefore, by defining the grammar in BNF we are programming the compiler system.

The compiler system uses the BNF rules to examine an input statement written in speedcode, analyze the speedcode, and produce kludgecode as illustrated by the streamlining examples. We can automate the blueprint production step between speedcode and kludgecode by using the practical features of BNF. This is discussed in the next section.

Scan, Parse, and Other Orthodontia

The BNF description of a programming language gives all rules necessary for the generation of any sentence (statement) of a language. A compiler on the other hand, must do the opposite. Given a statement from a language, the compiler must "recognize" the statement, break it into its parts-of-speech, and produce the semantics of the statement in some output form. Each one of these steps has a specific name, and a specific place in the compiler.

1. Scan: recognize the statement
2. Parse: break into parts-of-speech
3. Code generation: produce semantics

The scanner of a language usually reads each character of every line, combines the characters into low-level terminals (like variables, constants, and operators), and replaces them by their *tokens*. A token is a symbol used to represent another symbol. The parts-of-speech are replaced by their tokens in order to reduce the storage requirements for mnemonic tables, etc.

We define the scanner as a token function, T. For example,

$$30 = T (\text{<variable>})$$
$$40 = T (\text{<constant>})$$

In the examples, above, the token function produced numeric values in place of the parts-of-speech. The illustrations below employ the full non-terminal names and notation, but the reader should remember that in a real-world compiler, only tokens are managed.

The scanner performs a limited amount of parsing. Parsing is the process of *reducing* an input statement to smaller and smaller pieces. Each piece corresponds directly with a production rule of the grammar. In fact, the LHS of a production used to reduce an input statement is the name attached to the piece of input. Hence, an input is reduced to a "primary," say, by the production rule defining "primary" as a "variable" or "constant."

The code generation step is mixed in with the parse step. At each parse reduction we produce kludgecode corresponding with the operation to be performed by the statement being reduced. This step is illustrated in greater detail in the next section on kludgecode generation.

Let us return now to the scan and parse steps of a compiler. Suppose we use the BNF rules given in the previous section to reduce the following expression.

$$B/C + D*E$$

The method used here is called a "bottom-up" algorithm. That is, we begin at the bottom of a tree-like diagram and work up to the root of the tree. This will become apparent in what follows.

The bottom-up algorithm works by searching the BNF rules at the same time it scans the input expression. When the B is scanned, the algorithm searches the RHS of every BNF statement looking for a match between <simple variable> and the production.

$$B \underline{\quad\quad} \text{<simple variable>}$$

If an RHS is found which exactly matches the pattern <variable>, the right-hand-side is reduced by replacing it with the corresponding LHS. This is possible with production rule #9. Hence we "grow" the tree.

B — <simple variable> — <variable>

Again, the RHSs of the productions are searched looking for a <variable>. We locate a match in production rule #8. The tree is grown further.

B — <simple variable> — <variable> — <primary>

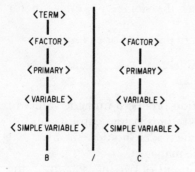

Fig. 8.1 Partial parse of the expression B/C + D*E.

Continuing the search, we locate a <primary>in production rule #7, and reduce it to <factor>.

B — <simple variable> — <variable> — <primary> — <factor>

After another search we locate <term>in productions #5 and #6. We could reduce the <term> to a <sum> using production #5, but look at rule #6. In rule #6 the third line contains a / symbol. This symbol matches the next input from the scanner. The scanner looks ahead one token to see a token that matches the RHS of a production.

A bottom-up algorithm is called "single look ahead" whenever the next input token is needed to choose between two or more possible reductions. We could have performed either reduction (#5 or #6), but given the look ahead token /, the decision is to wait until rule #6 is completely matched. Thus, we temporarily suspend the growth of the tree at the point shown in Fig. 8.1.

Figure 8.1 shows the result obtained by growing the tree up to the highest point possible by reducing an RHS to an LHS whenever possible. Each time a reduction phase is halted due to the inability to continue

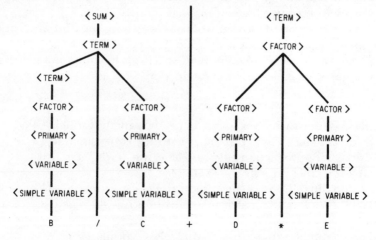

Fig. 8.2 More parsing of B/C + D*E.

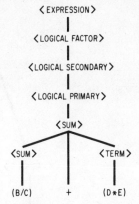

Fig. 8.3 Final reductions to parse B/C + D*E.

(there are *no* matches), we begin another branch of the tree. In Fig. 8.1 we have had to start two new branches with leaves of / and c.

The state of affairs in Fig. 8.1 shows that an RHS of the form <term>/<factor> is needed to perform a reduction. We search all BNF rules and find that rule #6 matches. The reduction produces a sub-tree as shown in Fig. 8.2. Continuing the same policy gives the sub-trees shown in Fig. 8.2 after scanning for the remaining input tokens.

The state of Fig. 8.2 is reducible to the "goal" token <expression> by additional reductions as before. The result is illustrated in the abbreviated "super-tree" shown in Fig. 8.3.

The reduction-search algorithm used in bottom-up parsing is very simple to implement in a machine with a pushdown stack. The process is as follows:

1. Initialize the stack, scanner, and BNF rules.
2. Repeat the following until the stack underflows:
   (a) Scan the input and deliver a token.
   (b) Push the token onto the stack.
   (c) Search the RHS list for a match between one or more elements on the stack, and a production rule.
   (d) If a reduction is possible, reduce the stack by replacing the RHS by its LHS equivalent. Repeat this step until no additional reductions are possible. (This involves pulling the stack.)
3. If no reductions are possible, the stack is not empty, and the input is completely scanned, then the statement must be incorrect (faulty grammar).

This algorithm builds a stack in place of a tree. The trees given in Figs. 8.1, 8.2, and 8.3 are mere aids to understanding the method; they don't have to exist. Hence, we construct a stack full of tokens, and perform the searches and reductions until the input is exhausted and the

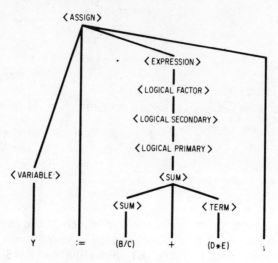

Fig. 8.4 Parse of Y:= B/C + D*E.

stack is emptied. Any deviation from the process indicates an error in the speedcode program.

Observe the independence of the bottom-up algorithm. It works for other languages besides speedcode (as specified by their BNF description, and for other microprocessors). Thus, the bottom-up, single look ahead algorithm is quite general, and powerful. Most speedcode-like languages are compiled by bottom-up algorithms.

Next, we must generate kludgecode from the parser. This is done by proper insertion of code generation algorithms into the BNF rules. In the next section we modify the bottom-up algorithm to handle code generation.

Kludgecode Generation

We can generate kludgecode for any microprocessor by careful insertion of code generators into the bottom-up algorithm. The secret is to place the appropriate generators at each reduction rule. That is, each line of the BNF description corresponds with one or more lines of kludgecode.

Suppose we examine the BNF productions that impact the parser and code generator for the expression below.

$$Y:= B/C + D*E;$$

We parsed the right-hand-side of this statement in Fig. 8.3. All we need to complete the reduction is the following production.

13. <assign> ::= <variable> := <expression>;

This rule is used to reduce the tree of Fig. 8.3 to a root (at the "top") consisting of "<assign>" (see Fig. 8.4). Notice the additional limbs needed to do this.

We know from the earlier chapters that 6800 kludgecode equivalent of the assignment statement is as follows:

```
*        Y:= B/C + D*E;
         LDA   A   B
         PSH   A              **push B
         LDA   A   C
         PSH   A              **push C
         JSR       QUOT       **B/C
         LDA   A   D
         PSH   A              **push D
         LDA   A   E
         PSH   A              **push E
         JSR       MULT       **D*D
         PUL   B
         PUL   A
         ABA                  **B/C + D*E
         PSH   A
         PUL   A
         STA   A   Y          **Y:= B/C + D*E
*  done
```

How can we insert the proper code generators into the BNF so that every time a reduction is done by the computer, we obtain kludgecode that always works, properly? The following modified BNF statements do exactly what we want them to do. Furthermore, they *always* do what we want done!

```
5'.  <sum>  ::=  <term>
            ::=  <sum> + <term> : GEN( PUL   B
                                       PUL   A
                                       ABA
                                       PSH   A)
            ::=  <sum> — <term> : GEN( PUL   B
                                       PUL   B
                                       SBA
                                       PSH   A)
            ::=  —<term> : GEN(        PUL   A
                                       NEG   A
                                       PSH   A)
            ::=  + <term>
```

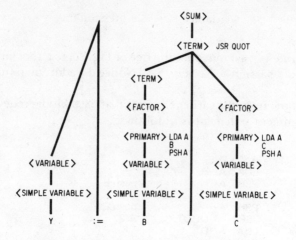

Fig. 8.5 Code reduction at each reduction.

6'. <term> ::= <factor>
          ::= <term> * <factor> : **GEN**(JSR mult)
          ::= <term> / <factor> : **GEN**(JSR quot)

9'. <primary> ::= <variable> : **GEN**(LDA   A   <variable>
                              PSH   A   )
          ::= <constant> : **GEN**(LDA   A   # <constant>
                              PSH   A   )

13'. <assign> ::= <variable>
          := <expression>; : **GEN**(PUL   A
                                   STA   A   <variable>)

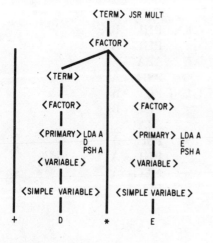

Fig. 8.6 Code generation for MULTIPLY.

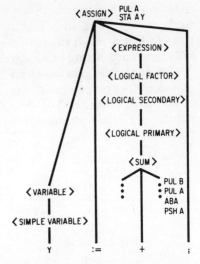

Fig. 8.7 Final steps of code generation.

Now, if we perform the bottom-up parse algorithm and generate the code indicated in each **GEN** command, then the outputs taken together, produce the desired kludgecode. The sequence of snapshots in Figs. 8.5, 8.6, and 8.7 illustrate what happens.

The kludgecode generator produces the code we have used throughout this book for each construct: **if–then–else, while, procedure, var.** The exact details are left as an exercise for the reader. It is necessary to point out several important details, however.

Each code generation involving a label must either generate a unique new label for branch destinations, or "remember" a previously generated label. Consider the code generation for an **if–then–else** expression, for example.

The compiler must include a "random label" generator that produces unique labels upon demand. If the procedure name followed by a dot number is used:

nam.#

then the labels are made unique by counting. Other methods of label generation may be used so long as the labels are unique.

The computer must also maintain a symbol table similar to the tables used by the assembler (see earlier chapter). The symbol table is used for computing values and retrieving names when needed.

Finally, we have overlooked the bookkeeping necessary to link procedures, set-up calls to the subscript subroutine, etc. These details are straightforward but messy to set up and include. The reader can do these in an analogous manner.

Once a compiler is implemented in a microprocessor development system a programmer can produce kludgecode at the speed of light. The code may be less compact than hand coded programs but they are more likely to be correct. After making the speedcode programs correct, make them fast. It is much easier to do both if work begins with an automatically generated listing of kludgecode.

A flashcode generator can be written as a program that reads the output of the computer and compacts each redundant segment of kludgecode. For example, back-to-back load and store operations can be eliminated, etc. These techniques were discussed in an earlier section on flashcode.

9

Speedcode at
Warp-Factor Five

An ancient prisoner was punished by having to roll a huge stone to the top of a mountain, only to have the stone tumble to the valley. He spent each day pushing the weight to the top, then watched as it crashed to the bottom. This went on for many years before a thought occurred to him.

At night the prisoner devised a wind-powered lever. His windmill was designed to pump water to the top of the mountain. The water was to rush to the river winding its way through the valley, and in the process, turn a giant paddle wheel. The paddle wheel would turn a pully, the pully would pull a rope, and the rope would pull the stone to the top of the mountain.

Ten years passed before his invention was turned into reality. His invention was about to be put to use when the king granted him a pardon.

Moral. A dream can help to make reality easier to tolerate. (For the hardcore computer engineer, thinking of the perfect machine may not be a waste of time after all, if it helps you to put up with the shortcomings of the machine you have.)

* * *

Flying High with a High-Level Language

In the age of million dollar programs and ten dollar computers it is absurd to write programs directly in kludgecode. Furthermore, it is absurd to worry about streamlining speedcode into kludgecode and ultimately into flashcode by manual craftsmanship. Manual streamlining is less reliable, less efficient in human terms, and produces a less intelligible product to maintain. In short, we are well rewarded for applying the techniques of the previous chapter to the automatic production of speedcode at the speed of light. Indeed, speedcode translation can be done by a computer program called a compiler.

Various microprocessor manufacturers provide a kind of speedcode language suited for systems implementation programming. We will survey one such language originally developed by William McKeeman and modified by Intel Corp. for use with 8-bit microprocessors like the Intel 8008, 8080, 8085, and in slightly modified form for the 16-bit 8086. The PL/M (programming language for microprocessors) language is a derivative of PL/I and XPL.

In PL/M a program is written as a collection of procedures, each procedure consists of simple one-line statements, or compound statements containing one or more statements. Actually, a procedure may be either *external* (defined outside the program like a subroutine in assembly language), or *internal* (defined inside the program so it can share variables with the "main" program). The general structure of a PL/M program is shown below. Note that every compound statement begins with a **do** keyword and terminates with an **end** statement.

```
program: do;
         _____
         _____
         _____
         declare variables used by all
         procedures . . . these are called "global"
         _____
         _____
         _____
         declare external procedures
         _____
         _____
         declare and insert the code for internal
         procedures . . . along with their "local" data.
         _____
         _____
         give code for main program calculations
         and "calls" to other procedures.
         _____
         _____
         _____
         end program;
```

The most interesting feature of the PL/M structure is the use of global and local data. A local data variable is declared within the module (a module is a procedure or compound statement containing a declaration of local variables) of its use. We could *nest* modules so that an inner module inherits the data from an outer module.

```
A: procedure;
            declare BUFFER (130) byte;
            declare INDEX address;
            declare LF literally 'OAH';
            declare CR literally 'ODH';
```

```
    ─────
    ─────
    ─────
B:  procedure (NUMBER, START, STOP);
    declare NUMBER address;
    declare LINE based START byte;
    declare SWITCH byte data (OOH);
    declare (START, STOP) address;

    ─────
    end B;

    ─────
    call B (INDEX, 0010H, 0020H);
    ─────
end A
```

The abstracted program text above shows how the variables declared in module A are also accessible by statements in module B, because B is an inner module. Thus, procedure B is an internal procedure sharing the variables BUFFER, INDEX, LF, CR with procedure A. The variables local to B are *not* accessible from outside B, however. Therefore, in order to pass values computed inside module B back to module A, we are forced to use the parameter list of module B.

Procedure B is activated by "calling" B, as shown in the remaining code of procedure A. The hexadecimal constants 10 and 20 are passed as 16-bit values to formal variables START and STOP (see the parameter list of procedure B).

The code above also demonstrates the data types of PL/M (especially for the 8080 and 8085 microcomputers). The array BUFFER consists of 130 bytes, numbered from zero to 129. Each byte is an 8-bit data element, hence to get 16-bit addresses (say to use the HL-register pair on the 8080), we must declare variables as addresses. The INDEX, NUMBER, START, and STOP variables are each 16-bit values.

Constants such as CR and LF are declared as LITERALLY "0A" and "0D," hex, as shown. They are variables that cannot be altered during calculation. Variable LINE is unique in the example above because it is a byte-valued variable whose address is stored in START. Hence the location of LINE is based on the value of START. This type of data structure is useful for processing pointers to data. Finally, the DATA attribute of SWITCH illustrates how a variable is initialized (00 hex) at the same time it is declared. The initialization may be overridden by an assignment calculated later in the program.

The PL/M language also provides a powerful data structure facility whereby the programmer can construct chains of data, each element of the chain may consist of mixed data types. For instance, to describe the internal registers of the 8080 microprocessor, we can declare a **structure** REG, to be the collection of working registers.

```
     $ EJECT
237  1   INTEGER:    PROCEDURE;            /* CONVERT ASCII STRING TO BINARY NUMBER */
238  2               DECLARE HOLD BYTE;
239  2               IRPTR=0;
240  2               DO WHILE (BUFFER(BUFFPTR)>='0') AND (BUFFER(BUFFPTR)<='9');
241  3                   IF IRPTR<1024 THEN
242  3                       DO;
243  4                           HOLD=BUFFER(BUFFPTR)-'0';
244  4                           IRPTR=10*IRPTR+HOLD;
245  4                       END;
246  3                   BUFFPTR=BUFFPTR+1;
247  3               END;
248  2               IF IRPTR>1023 THEN CALL ERRMESS(10);
250  2               RETURN;
251  2   END INTEGER;
```

Fig. 9.1 Convert ASCII string to a binary number.

```
declare REG structure (
          (A, B, C, D, E, H, L) byte,
          (BC, DE, HL)        address,
          (PC, SP)            address);
```

The structure type allows a variety of more sophisticated data structures. For instance, suppose we declare a variable with 100 elements, each element is a node of a "tree" containing a LEFT pointer to a left subtree, and a RIGHT pointer to a right subtree. The PL/M structure is described to the PL/M compiler as shown below. Access to a structure variable is shown by the dot notation.

```
declare TREE (100) based ROOT structure (
              KEY byte,
              (LEFT, RIGHT) address);
TREE (INDEX).LEFT = OLD;
```

The PL/M language closely resembles the speedcode used throughout this book. The control structures include *basic* actions, *looping* actions, and *choice* actions, for example, and a case select construct for convenience.

```
do case flag;
      /* do when flag = 0 * /   A = 10;
      /* do when flag = 1 * /   do;
                                    A = 10;
                                    B = 20;
                                 end;
      /* do when flag = 2 * /   B = 20;
```

Note in Fig. 9.1 and 9.2 the use of DO-END compound statements and the differences between PL/M and speedcode. Lets study the conversion procedure of Fig. 9.1, first.

An ASCII string is assumed stored in a string of bytes (BUFFER) beginning in location BUFFPTR and terminating when a nonnumeric character is found. The value of BUFFPTR is declared in an outer module, thus the INTEGER routine inherits BUFFPTR.

The resulting four digit number is stored in IRPTR. If it exceeds 1023, an error message is communicated to the user (ERRMESS(10)). Again, IRPTR is global to INTEGER because of the nesting assumed in Fig. 9.1.

The **do while** loop is repeated until a nonnumeric character is found. Since the comparison is done against strings "0" and "9," the PL/M language does *not* rely upon encoding of either "0" or "9." Thus, the string in BUFFER may be either ASCII, EBCDIC, or some other display code and the procedure will operate correctly (assuming the codes are ordered).

The conversion routine in Fig. 9.2 does the exact opposite of Fig. 9.1, but it is more elaborate because it must consider the possibility of leading zeros in the binary-to-decimal conversion. Up to 10 characters may be produced by PACK in locations BUFFPTR to BUFFPTR + 9. These locations are initially "cleared" to contain blanks.

```
     $ EJECT

72   1   PACK:     PROCEDURE (NUMBER,BUFFSTRT,BUFFPTR);        /* CONVERT BINARY NUMBER TO ASCII STRING */
73   2             DECLARE NUMBER ADDRESS;
74   2             DECLARE BUFFSTRT ADDRESS;
75   2             DECLARE BUFFER BASED BUFFSTRT(1) BYTE;
76   2             DECLARE BUFFPTR BYTE;
77   2             DECLARE CONSTANT ADDRESS;
78   2             DECLARE HOLD BYTE;
79   2             DECLARE SWITCH BYTE;
80   2             DECLARE (I,J) BYTE;
81   2             SWITCH=0;          /* SUPPRESS LEADING ZEROS */
82   2             DO I=BUFFPTR TO BUFFPTR+9;      /* CLEAR BUFFER */
83   3                 BUFFER(I)=' ';
84   3             END;
85   2             J=0;
86   2             CONSTANT=10000;
87   2             DO I=0 TO 3;       /* PROCESS 4 DIGIT NUMBER */
88   3.                HOLD=(NUMBER MOD CONSTANT)/(CONSTANT/10);
89   3                 IF (HOLD<>0) OR (SWITCH=1) THEN
90   3                     DO;
91   4                         BUFFER(BUFFPTR+J)=HOLD+'0';
92   4                         J=J+1;
93   4                         SWITCH=1;
94   4                     END;
95   3                 CONSTANT=CONSTANT/10;
96   3             END;
97   2             IF BUFFER(BUFFPTR)=' ' THEN BUFFER(BUFFPTR)='0';
99   2             RETURN;
100  2         END PACK;
```

Fig. 9.2 Convert binary number to an ASCII string.

The conversion routine starts by dividing the binary number by 1000, producing a remainder. The MOD function is the divide function of PL/M that returns a remainder rather than a quotient.

As soon as a nonzero digit is obtained, SWITCH is set to one indicating that zero-suppression is no longer needed. Subsequent remainders are obtained from division by CONSTANT = 100, 10, and finally 1.

A final test in PACK is used to make sure a zero is returned when *every* digit in the converted number turned out to be a leading zero. In this case SWITCH is never set to a one, and yet we must return at least one zero to BUFFER (BUFFPTR).

PL/M handles input and output with reserved *pseudovariables* called INPUT (device #), and OUTPUT (device #). Thus, to obtain a value from part 02H and output it to part 05H, we would use the INPUT and OUTPUT pseudovariables in an assignment statement.

OUTPUT (05H) = INPUT (02H);

PL/M has many other features not described here. In fact, these features are natural extensions of the basic concept of speedcode, and are quickly mastered once the concepts suggested here are mastered. The PL/M compiler is a program (also written in PL/M) that usually runs on an Intel development system with diskette, and 64k of main memory. The READ and WRITE procedures for diskette I/O are provided in a library of external procedures. The user program must declare these routines as external procedures before using them.

```
OPEN:   procedure ("parameters") external;
CLOSE:  procedure ("parameters") external;
READ:   procedure ("parameters") external;
WRITE:  procedure ("parameters") external;
```

Also, it may be helpful to be able to manipulate the address of variables rather than their values, directly. Thus, for example, the PACK procedure is called with an address as a parameter instead of a value. The dot prefix is used here to denote "the address of."

call PACK (COUNT, .PTR, 0);

This invocation passes a 16-bit number stored in COUNT, the address of PTR, and the 16-bit index value "zero" to internal procedure PACK, see Fig. 9.2.

PL/M is a speedcode designed to reduce program production costs, maintenance costs, and errors in programs. It does so by reducing the number of "parts" needed to put a software system together. Each PL/M statement, for example, produces anywhere from one to ten assembler-language statements. If an average "gain" of five is obtained by employing PL/M, then we can expect software production to be five times more effective. Actually, the gain may be greater due to the exponentially increasing complexity of systems consisting of many parts.

Speedcode Machines in the Sky

If high-level languages such as PL/M are so great an advantage, then why are computers equipped with assembler languages? Furthermore, if the code produced by a speedcode is inefficient, then why not use assembler language for all programming?

The answer to the first question is due mainly to tradition. The very early software engineers knew too little of formal languages and programming to insist on powerful tools like PL/M. Hence, symbolic machine language gained a strong foothold. Indeed the influence of assembly language is difficult to overcome in spite of the obvious drawbacks it provides.

In the age of million dollar programs, and ten dollar computers, the obvious solution to inefficient high level language code is to ignore the "inefficiencies." By the time a large-scale software system is implemented in its most efficient form, the basic technology of microprocessors will have advanced to the point where the efficient implementation is obsolete. On the contrary, a reliable, cheap, inefficient implementation in PL/M, say, will run faster, cheaper, and more reliably on the microprocessor of the future than *any* assembler-language implementation. This rash conjecture is supported by the example given in this section.

The Intel 8086 is a 16-bit processor that runs PL/M object code, 8080 and 8085 source code, and performs both 8-bit and 16-bit operations. It is a processor (actually two processors, internally) that executes "inefficient" PL/M programs written for the 8080, and 8085 microprocessors much faster than those same programs could execute if they were tuned for 8080 flashcode.

The 8086 is a PL/M-directed microcomputer. That is, many features of the 8086 are designed to support PL/M. The philosophy of the design is this: when the programs are inefficient, change the computer to make the programs run better. In short, we have come full circle in computer technology. Hardware is soft (can be easily changed), and software is hard (cannot be easily changed). When the application requires a 16-bit data width and speed, then change the processor, not the programs!

INTEL 8086 Specifications	
ALU width	16 bits
Addressing	1,048,576 bytes
I/O	64k ports
Clock speed	200 ns and 125 ns
Memory speed	800 ns and 500 ns

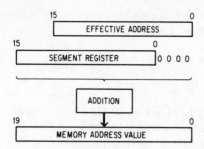

Fig. 9.3 The 1-MB addressability of the 8086.

The 8086 is 7 to 12 times more powerful than the 8080A, for example. Thus, if we run 8080A programs on the 8086 we would expect from 700% to 1200% increased performance. This increase certainly removes the question of inefficency of programs from the software development picture, but there is more to come. The 8086 is also a "high-level machine," because many PL/M operations done on the 8080 require many instructions, but when done on the 8086 require only one or two instructions.

The memory of an 8086 system is segmented into 64k byte segments. Each 16-bit address generated by an instruction fetch and/or data reference is extended by adding a shifted segment register to produce 20-bits of addressability, see Fig. 9.3.

The 8086 contains a *superset* of the 8080 registers. In addition, the multisegment main memory is managed by four segment registers, see Fig. 9.4. The complete set of 8086 registers consists of four general/special purpose working registers, four segment registers, four pointer/index registers, the program counter, and the (extended) flag register.

These registers make PL/M data structures easy to implement. For example, declaration of simple variables, arrays, and based structures is a signal for the PL/M compiler to use the 8086 registers in the following ways.

> *Simple variable:* Use direct access mode.

> *Array variable:* Set up the array subscript value in register SI (source index). Generate the array base location as part of the instruction. During execution, the array base address is added to the SI register to come up with an effective address.

> *Based variable:* Simple variables are located by placing the value of the pointer variable into the BX register. The BX register is used as a pointer to the based variable. If the based variable is an array, the pointer variable value is put into BX and then access is done as before for an array.

> *Program (Procedure) Activation:* The stack pointed to by register SP is marked by loading BP with the current value

of SP. The 8086 assembler code generated by PL/M is
shown for a simple case, below.

```
call PROC  (X, Y)   ;**/* PL/M call */
     PUSH  X         ;**pass X, Y on TOS
     PUSH  Y         ;**
     CALL  proc      ;**call internal proc
```

This sequence causes entry into the procedure
and in the process sets up the pointers needed
to get back.

```
PROC: procedure (A, B)   ;**/* PL/M version */
      PUSH  BP           ;**save BP on TOS
      MOV   BP, SP       ;**copy SP into BP
```

This sequence causes the stack to be marked (for
return) by BP upon entry into the procedure.
The return sequence discards the values placed
on the stack.

```
return: MOV  SP, BP   ;**restore SP
        POP  BP       ;**discard BP
        RET  4        ;**discard 4 bytes . . .
                      ;**of X and Y values
```

Fig. 9.4 The register files of the 8086. (The 8080 allocation is shown in parentheses.)

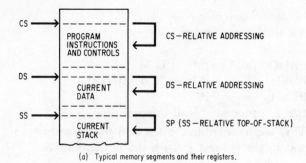

(a) Typical memory segments and their registers.

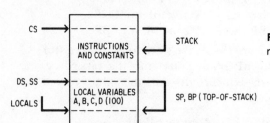

(b) Configuration at entry to program HULK.

Fig. 9.5 Demonstration of 8086 register use.

The following PL/M source code is formulated into 8086 assembler code (speedcode-to-kludgecode) by the PL/M compiler. Suppose program HULK is compiled:

```
HULK: do;
        declare (A, B, C) word, D(100) word, L literally '5';
        do while   D(A + B) < D(A + B + 1);
            D(C) = D(C) + 1;
        end;
        ;
        if A < B + (L — 1) then A = A * 2;
                            else  A = A + 1;
        end HULK;
```

This program does little of importance, but it illustrates the levels of code streamlining that are automatically done by the compiler.

First, the registers are set up, and space is allocated in the stack segment for the "local" variables, A, B, C, and D. Note that D is an array of words, while the other variables are single words, each. The literal variable L is a constant and does not require storage in main memory. Instead, L is generated as a constant contained within the program code, see below.

Figure 9.5a illustrates the general register assignments for mapping the 8086 main memory. The compiled object code is stored in a code segment designated by register CS. The data is stored in locations (DS) through (DS + length), while the pushdown stack is referenced through register SS. Note that the top-of-stack register contains a displacement value offset from SS.

The compiler generates code to set-up the register as shown in Fig. 9.5b. This is done after the DECLARE statement.

```
HULK: DO;
       DECLARE (A,B,C) WORD, D(100) WORD, L LITERALLY '5';
       ;
          CLI                     **disable system interrupts
          MOV    SS, CS:STACK     **locate a constant
                                  **at location STACK, within segment
                                  **pointed at by CS, and copy it into
                                  **the SS register. Thus, establish
                                  **the stack segment for this program.
          MOV    SP, LOCALS       **increment stack pointer
                                  **so that it bypasses local variables
                                  **on the stack.
          MOV    BP, SP           **duplicate SP in BP register
          PUSH   SS               **copy SS . . .
          POP    DS               **. . . into DS
          STI                     **enable system interrupts
       DO WHILE D(A + B) < D(A + B + 1);
       ;
@3     :
          MOV    BX, B            **load B into register BX
          ADD    BX, A            **(A + B) into register BX
          SHL    BX, 1            **2*(A + B) to get WORD address
          MOV    SI, B            **load B into register SI
          ADD    SI, A            **(A + B) into register SI
          SHL    SI, 1            **2*(A + B) to get WORD address
          MOV    AX, D [BX]       **get D(A + B) into register AX
          CMP    AX, D [SI + 2]   **D(A + B) < D(A + B + 1)  ??
          JB     $+5H             **yes, continue loop; skip S bytes
          JMP    @4               **no, exit loop at label @4
```

This piece of kludgecode uses two registers to index into array D. The subscript value (A + B) is computed and stored in 16-bit general register BX and the value of (A + B) is computed a second time and stored in register SI. Since the data is declared **word** (2 bytes each), the offset address is shifted left one bit to effectively multiply the subscript values by two.

The labels @3 and @4 are used to delimit the beginning and end of the **do while** loop.

The next statement is compiled as usual.

```
D(C) = D(C) + 1;
;
       MOV    BX, C        **compute the subscript . . .
       SHL    BX, 1        **. . . of element D(C)
       MOV    AX, D[BX]     **copy D(C) into register AZ
       ADD    AX, 1        **increment D(C) . . .
       MOV    BX, C        **recompute the subscript . . .
```

```
SHL   BX, 1          **. . . for second D(C)
MOV   D[BX], AX      **store D(C) + 1 into D(C)
```

The loop terminates with an **end** statement and reenters the loop at label @ 3.

```
end;
;
      JMP      @3      **re-enter loop
@4:                    **no, exit loop
```

Next, we see how PL/M compiles the *choice* action construct. In this case, L is a literal (self-defined constant). Thus, (L — 1) is also a literal which can be immediately plugged into the program.

```
if A < B + (L — 1);
;
      MOV   AX, B        **computer B + 4 . . .
      ADD   AX, 4H       **and place in AX
      CMP   A, AX        **A < B + 4 ??
      JB    $ + 5H       **yes, skip over next op-code
      JMP   @1           **no, do ELSE clause
;
then A = A*2;
      MOV   AX, A        **perform a quick . . .
      SHL   AX, 1        **. . . multiply of 2*A,
      MOV   A, AX        **and stuff into A
      JMP   @2           **skip over ELSE clause
@1:
;
else A = A + 1;·
;
      MOV   AX, A        **compute A = . . .
      ADD   AX, 1H       **. . . A + 1
      MOV   A, AX        **store into A
@2:
;
end HULK;
;
```

Clearly the kludgecode for HULK is inefficient. For example, the common expressions (A + B) and D(C) are computed more often than needed. The jump commands are less efficient than an assembler programmer is capable of writing. Is it possible for PL/M to produce flash-code by analyzing the code above in a manner similar to what a programmer does?

Indeed, PL/M can streamline object code in a manner similar to hand coding. The PL/M compiler is slowed down significantly by streamlining, however. Yet, when a programmer's time is more valuable than a ten-dollar computer, it makes sense to streamline 8086 kludgecode.

The PL/M programmer can request streamline optimization. When OPTIMIZE(1) is requested, the object code is reduced by common expression elimination, reduction of constant expressions, etc. When, OPTIMIZE(2) is specified, the PL/M compiler performs a lengthy analysis of the flow of control through the body of the program and its subprocedures. Short jumps are analyzed by OPTIMIZE(2), for example.

Suppose we re-compile HULK using OPTIMIZE(1). Instead of generating 120 bytes of object code, the result is a shorter (faster) program of 86 bytes.

```
DO WHILE D(A + B) < D(A + B + 1);
;
@3:
      MOV   BX, B
      ADD   BX, A
      SHL   BX, 1
      MOV   AX, D[BX]         **get D(A + B)
      CMP   AX, D[BX + 2]     **get and compare . . .
                             **D[A + B + 1]
      JB    $ + 5H
      JMP   @4
```

The common subexpression (A + B) has been eliminated in the streamlined version, above. We can also shorten the increment instructions for computing D(C) + 1.

```
D(C) = D(C) + 1;
;
      MOV   BX, C
      SHL   BX, 1
      ADD   D[BX], 1H        **increment D(C)
```

We can do a similar streamlining of the A = A*2 expression, see below.

```
THEN A = A*2;
;
      SHL   A, 1      **A = A*2
```

Finally, the increment expression for variable A can be shortened.

```
ELSE A = A + 1;
;
      ADD   A, 1H        **increment A.
```

The OPTIMIZE(2) analysis is capable of reducing the flashcode even further by eliminating excess branches. The following reductions produce a HULK program of 74 bytes instead of 86.

Replace;

```
    JB      $ + 5H
    JMP     @4
```

with the negative test and branch:

```
    JNB     @4
```

This substitution is done in two places in HULK. Hence, the result is a program nearly as compact as any written by a human programmer.

We have illustrated two important concepts in software engineering of microcomputer systems:

1. High level languages are proven tools for reducing programming costs.
2. Compilers are capable of streamlining speedcode into efficient flashcode in a manner suitable for fast, efficient, and reliable program execution in microcomputers.

In the age of microcomputer software development where ten dollar computers require million dollar programs, it is absurd to ignore the power and efficiency of speedcode in the development of microcomputer software.

The final section of this chapter is pure speculation. In closing, the author takes the reader on a trip into a possible future where hardware is designed to match the software task ahead.

Where the Author Takes a Trip

In the near future computers will become increasingly sophisticated in order to lower the software development costs of an overall application. In the LSI age, hardware is a minor cost item, but software is a major cost item. Is it possible to shift some of the software onto the hardware?

The "hardware shift" is a trend in computing. Whenever the cost of a hardware component becomes ridiculously low, that component becomes standardized. For example, UART (universal asynchronous, receive and transmit) circuits are used to communicate serial data between a processor and a peripheral device. Since UART circuits have become very inexpensive due to LSI, most UART chips have conformed to a uniform standard.

Unfortunately, software components have yet to become standardized. Many engineers believe that the computer industry should agree on standards for modules, e.g. searching, sorting, file structures and access mechanisms, and programming languages. This approach fails because it is unlikely that the competitive computer industry will agree to a single way of doing the same things. Hence many software components that should be standard components are still "nonstandard."

Software components will become standardized when their cost is reduced to the point where it is no longer profitable to reinvent the "wheel." When the cost is ridiculously low, then the ad hoc standard will be enforced by the buyers. Few software engineers will venture to develop a file structure and access subsystem when it can be purchased in its "hardware manifestation" for $10.

The implication of low cost software modules is the rise of "LSI software." A standard software component such as a SORT package is combined with a microprocessor and ROM to create a SORT subsystem. The SORT subsystem is physically plugged into the computer system. Whenever a sort is needed by an application programmer, it is called like any other subprocedure, but in reality the LSI SORT routine will be a hardware chip.

A system of LSI modules suggests a distributed network of computers. The network is "tightly coupled" if the components are in close proximity and highly coordinated by a monitoring module. The network is "loosely coupled" if the modules are accessed via a communications network. We will discuss tightly coupled systems, only.

In a tightly coupled system, all modules must cooperate in a carefully orchestrated sequence to gain the maximum possible throughput. Exactly how much orchestration is done is a subject of considerable research. However, several promising approaches have been initially explored. We will illustrate the "data flow" model of distributed control. Keep in mind, however, that other approaches are possible.

Suppose we study a simplified example of a software module that searches an array of elements looking for a value equal to "key." The module returns zero if "key" is not in array "x[1 . . n]," and returns the location of "key," otherwise.

This module can be implemented in two forms. The "control dual" form is the method used throughout this book. If we use the control dual, then we get a speedcode implementation as shown below.

```
LOOK: procedure (x:ARRAY[I . . n] of words, n, key: word) word;
          var  i: word;
          i:= 1;
          while (i ≤ n) loop;
                  if (key = x [i] ) then return (i) end if;
                  i:= i + 1;
          end loop;
          return (0);
      end LOOK
```

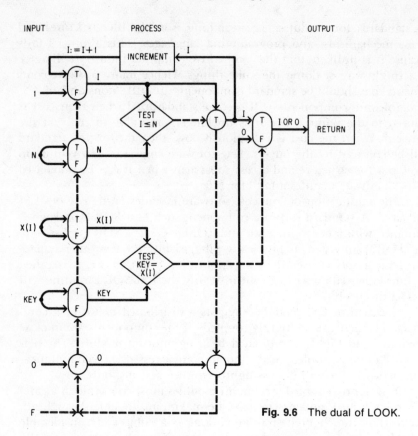

Fig. 9.6 The dual of LOOK.

    The control dual has a twin called the "dataflow dual." In the dataflow dual representation, we see how parallel execution of a network of subcomponents can speed the execution of this program. Figure 9.6 shows the dataflow program equivalent to LOOK. Note how we have organized the flow of data from its INPUT state, through its PROCESSing, and out to the final value. Thus, data flows from left-to-right in a dataflow program.

    In Fig. 9.6, each variable is shown as a label on a solid line. Each control line is dotted, while each active component is either a decision "diamond," a computation block, or a round control node. The reader will have to orient his/her thinking to replace variables with actions, and calculations with "node firing." Suppose we follow the calculation through a few iterations.

    There is potential parallelism in the dataflow dual. In order to make sense out of Fig. 9.6 we must continually remember that a node can fire (execute its function) only when two conditions are met:

1. All inputs are present in the form of a token (marked incoming line).
2. The output line is cleared (has no token).

Initially we supply the values of all input variables and the control line is set to F (false). The inputs are attached to "deciders" with T and/or F states. A T-side accepts an input whenever it receives an input token and the input control line is true. The output of a decider is either a T-side token, or else an F-side token, depending on the control line value. Thus, in Fig. 9.6, the inputs are (from top to bottom):

$$I:= 1$$
$$N$$
$$X[I]$$
$$Key$$
$$0$$
$$False$$

Since all inputs are available as tokens to the test boxes, the next step of the dataflow program is to test (I:N) and (Key:X[I]), simultaneously. In the former case a T token is output along the dotted control line. In the latter case, either a T or an F is output to the control line leaving the test box.

The control values propagate at the speed of light. That is, there is no perceptible time delay in sending a control signal. Thus, the T value is sent to the T-side of all control boxes. This means that the gate for constants 1 and 0 are closed. The remaining values of I + 1, N, X[I], and key are ready to fire through the T-side of their deciders. However, they cannot fire until the output tokens from the previous steps are removed by flowing along the appropriate lines.

Suppose the output of "Key = X[I]" is F. The control line leading into the final decider box (before the RETURN) has a value of F. However, this decider cannot fire until the appropriate value (0 or I) is supplied. The only way zero can be supplied is by obtaining an F control from the test "I ≤ N." We get the T-side token for this decider each time we obtain a T from "I ≤ N." Sooner or later the value of I is supplied (go through the loop at least once) or the constant zero is allowed to flow through (the loop terminates). When this happens, the control line is tested to see if it is T or F. If T, the current value of I is output. If F, the constant zero is output.

The dataflow dual represents parallelism much more naturally than the control dual representation. Hence, dataflow dualisms are likely to gain wider acceptance as microprocessor components are distributed throughout tightly coupled systems.

Imagine a dataflow program wherein the active components are high-level software modules. Suppose, for example, each module were a

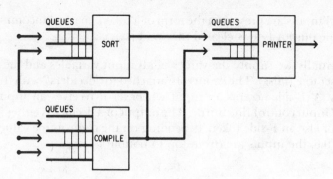

Fig. 9.7   A distributed network of LSI modules.

SOFT, FIND, INDEX FILE, COMPILE, or MATHPACK LSI module. The distribution of function in such a system would allow greater throughput if we coordinate their activation to take advantage of parallelism. Fig. 9.7 illustrates how the network might be implemented using waiting lines (queues) to store tokens.

The queues in Fig. 9.7 are necessary to keep the dataflow moving. The greater the parallelism the greater is throughput up to the limit of intermodule communication. Hence, the queues allow some congestion to occur without backing-up the entire work load of the system.

Many subtle problems remain for dataflow computers. Yet, the opportunity for low-cost systems is a strong motivating factor behind the work toward realizing dataflow computers. We turn now to an examination of a futuristic microcomputer that may become part of a dataflow system.

The Tagged Associative Memory Processor

The idea behind a tagged, associative-memory processor is very simple; elevate the level of the hardware so that programming is "easy" to do. By "elevate," we mean the machine is "language-directed." In the following futuristic microcomputer model, we attempt to incorporate features into the hardware that make programming in a high-level language less costly. In short we ask: What must we do to the processor to make speedcode easy to implement?

The first idea is to simplify programming by forcing the microprocessor to handle various forms of data, automatically. This is done at the expense of main memory, however, since we use tags to mark each cell of main memory with a flag designating the type of contents in the cell. A suggested list of types is given below for the hypothetical microprocessor of the future.

Type	*Meaning*
int	integer contents
real	floating point contents
undef	undefined contents
char	character contents
vec	single dimensional array
mat	matrix (2-D) array
ref	pointer to data elsewhere
label	label to code segment
stack	pushdown stack
q	first-come-first served queue
ps	parameter list for a procedure
proc	header for procedure environment
name	string for variable name
instr	executable instruction
formal	formal parameter list
ms	machine state word
ipt	interrupt vector
sema	semaphore for synchronization

The impact of tags on the running machine is quite extensive. There are two main contributions:

1. Programs are shorter and simpler because one instruction executes on any data type.
2. The system is more secure because the hardware checks for proper use; for example, data cannot be erroneously executed, mixed types are properly converted, etc.

The most obvious use for tags is in automatic compilation of code for speedcode. The example below illustrates the ease of generating code for a variety of data types.

```
var  A, B, C : integer
     X, Y, Z : real

     A:= B + C;
     X:= Y + Z;
```

The same sequence of executable kludgecode can be generated for both statements, above.

```
LOAD   B
ADD    C
STORE  A
```

```
LOAD    Y
ADD     Z
STORE   X
```

Furthermore, changing the types to vector, matrix, etc. does not alter the sequence of code generated because the microprocessor is able to determine what kind of operation to perform from the tags stored with the data. The data for the example, above, may appear in memory something like the following (symbolically).

Tag	Data value
int	A
int	B
int	C
real	X
real	Y
real	Z
undef	—
undef	—

In addition, the microprocessor refuses to execute instructions that attempt to alter memory of the wrong type. Hence, if the program erroneously accesses an "undef" region of memory, the arithmetic is not done. Instead, a type interrupt is generated.

The second idea we will use in designing a futuristic microprocessor is the associative store. An *associative memory* is a memory that can be addressed by its contents rather than a location value. The memory below is an example of association between values stored in memory and their attributes.

ATTRIBUTE	VALUE
cat	0
dog	25
name	'BOB'
5280	'MILE'

In an associative memory values are accessed by attribute. There is no concern for the location of a word, array, etc. and in some cases the association may produce multiple values.

ATTRIBUTE	VALUE
cat	0
dog	25
cat	15

We can now design the microcomputer architecture of the future. Indeed, the design is carried out in steps just as we advocate the design of software. We must set goals for the design, refine these goals into objectives, and finally, implement the objectives by architectural features. What exactly are the design goals of a futuristic microprocessor?

Goal 1. Support structured speedcode
Goal 2. Reduce compiler "effort."
Goal 3. Reduce execution "effort"
Goal 4. Reduce memory required
Goal 5. Incorporate protection mechanisms
Goal 6. Obey "good" design rules.

These goals are somewhat subjective, and often conflicting. For example, what do we mean by "good," and "effort?" Also, a goal that reduces memory may conflict with the goal of protection mechanisms. We must be careful to trade-off one feature for another during the refinement of these goals into a design.

We illustrate an "evolving" design methodology using the following speedcode example. This example does nothing useful except illustrate many of the features useful in nearly all language-directed computers.

```
MAIN: procedure
         var   A, B: real;
                  I: int;
         I:= 1;
         GET a;
         while (I < subx(A)) loop;
                  B:= B + float (I);
                  I:= 2*I;
         end loop;
         ;
         put A, B;
         ;
         subx: procedure (U: REAL) int;
                  var   B: int
                  ;
                  B:= (2*fix(U) + 1)/2;
                  return (B);
         end subx;
end MAIN
```

In addition, the design goals will be satisfied by solving problems associated with high-level languages of the past. The past is not always a good measure of the future, but it is the only data we have! Hence, we begin by refining the goals stated before.

Goal 2.1. When compiling a speedcode program use an associative store to keep the symbol table and a "high-level" instruction set for reduced lexical analysis and code generation.

Justification 2.1. Compiling a language is slow due to lexical analysis (65% in the past), and the corresponding symbol table look-up.

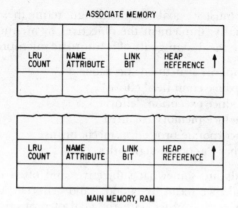

Fig. 9.8 An associative store for symbol tables.

As it turns out, associative memory is extremely expensive. There-fore, we must trade-off some associative store for some speed. This is done by combining the associative store with ordinary RAM. A least-recently-used tag (LRU) is used to keep the associative store full of the most likely entries to be asked for during a symbol table look-up.

The associative store is searched in one microcomputer memory cycle. If the NAME attribute is matched, then the symbol is located. However, if the NAME is not matched, then RAM must be searched in a slow linear fashion. The "hit ratio" of an associative store is a measure of the fractional utilization of the associative store. A hit ratio of 1.0 is perfect, while a ratio of 0.5 indicates that one-half of the table look-ups failed to be found in the associative store.

Hit ratios of 80%–90% are not unusual when associative stores with 1024 cells are employed. However, since we are storing a program's sym-bol table in the associative store, we have no control over the effective-ness of the store. Figure 9.8 illustrates the concept of an associative store when used to store a compiler's symbol table.

We note that there is a significant overhead associated with load-ing an associative store. This will not be of major concern unless the microprocessor is being shared by several processes. In other words, this design is not suited to multiprogrammed systems. Recall that we are dealing with a network of monoprogrammed processors rather than old fashioned single processor systems. In the age of ten dollar computers, we can well afford to duplicate processors rather than share them.

The items stored in the associative store are searched by comparing the search key with all NAME attributes in the store. The matching item is updated by adding one to the LRU count. If the LINK BIT is set, then the HEAP REFERENCE pointer is followed into RAM to access the variable, array, etc. The heap stored in RAM is managed by the LSI cir-cuitry using tags as suggested earlier.

Goal 3.1. Use tagged memory and pointers to build the heap in the RAM.

Justification 3.1. The hardware should support the heap store instead of the software.

We add a tag called ACCESS (designated ACL) to the types discussed earlier. The ACL entries provide the needed access protection requested in Goal 5. The chain of pointers shown in Fig. 9.9 show how the hardware must follow pointers along a linked list of heap entries in order to find all entries in an access list. We will discuss this in greater detail, later.

In Fig. 9.9 the heap consists of list headers and chains. The headers contain a pointer to data structures (arrays for example) or the actual value of the variable. For example, the value of variable "b" is stored in the header. Furthermore, each variable has an access list associated with it to provide protection. The acl pointer references a chain of ACL entries in the heap. These entries specify rews (read-only, execute-only, write-only, status-only) access. When used in combination, the rews flags define the kind of access permitted by each program or subprocedure.

In Fig. 9.9, the variable b has given rws access to the main program. This means the main program can read, write, and change the status of variable b. The ACL for the main program is given by the second entry in the heap header list. Thus main has permission to execute subprocedures "subr" and "float." After executing these two subprocedures, main may also read their values (passed back).

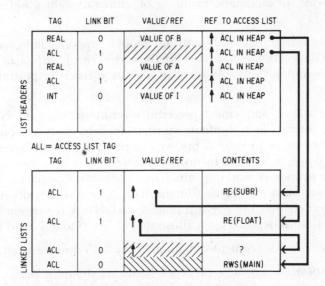

Fig. 9.9 The hardware supported heap.

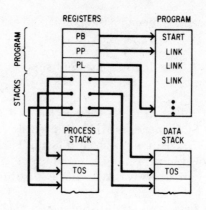

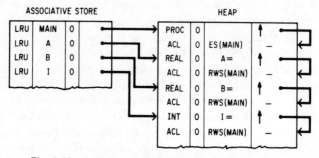

Fig. 9.10 Architecture of the future microprocessor.

Goal 3.2. Reduce load/store and push/pop operations, but still provide for automatic handling of temporary values and memory space.

Justification 3.2. The hardware should support "addressability," and data access as described briefly, above. Nearly 50% of an executing computer's time is spent in loading registers or pushing stack tops.

One way to implement powerful machine instructions is to use 3-address formats and eliminate registers entirely. This, of course, increases the size of programs, but we compensate for this by removing load/store operations, and incorporating tags.

The temporary working values are handled best by stacks. Processing is done on a data stack (intermediate values) while subprocedure invocation is handled by a return address stack. Thus, the system has two stacks of limited depth. This is illustrated in Fig. 9.10 discussed later.

Goal 3.3. Use segmented main memory with demand paging.

Justification 3.3. The processor hardware should manage its own main memory and not be limited by small physical storage.

This feature is immediate by using the associative store during execution of the compiled program. Instead of a NAME attribute, the table contains an address. Instead of a link bit, a "presence bit" is used to indicate the presence of the page containing the data. Finally, the reference pointer yields the address in physical storage.

Goal 5.1. Use tags to indicate access lists, and access rights to protect system security.

Justification 5.1. Access right protection should be handled at the same time that memory management and data access are handled.

This last feature is implemented by special linkage instructions in the processor.

The combined features are illustrated in the following compiled program.

```
MAIN procedure:
     start   MAIN = PROC, HEAP, acl = es (main)
```

This instruction tags "MAIN" as an object of type "proc," inserted into the heap, and with execute and status access given to main, itself.

```
var   A, B: real
      I:  int

      link   A = REAL, HEAP, acl = rws (MAIN)
      link   B = REAL, HEAP, acl = rws (MAIN)
      link   I = INT, HEAP, acl = rws (MAIN)
```

This declaration establishes symbol table entries for (A, B, I) and links them with their access lists. They give rws access to the main program. The result of these instructions is shown in Fig. 9.10 along with the system registers and stacks.

Suppose we compile the complete subr routine and study its linkage mechanisms. Note how access is granted to "MAIN" and local variables both, in the following.

```
SUBR: procedure (U:real)int;

      start   SUBR = INT PROC, HEAP, acl = es (MAIN)
      link    U = REAL, TOS, acl = rws (SUBR)
```

The entry "SUBR" is tagged as an integer procedure and placed in the heap. It is supplied an access list containing an entry for the main program. Since "MAIN" calls this routine, we have given execute-status rights to "MAIN." The formal parameter "U" is expected on the top of the data stack, hence a link is constructed to the top of the stack during execution. The formal parameter is defined by a value passed via the stack. The procedure "SUBR" is granted rws access rights to variable

"U." Hence, side-effects (write access) are allowed to occur to whatever actual parameter is linked to the top of stack. More on this later.

```
var  B: INT
     link  B = INT, HEAP, acl = rws (SUBR)
```

A new variable, local to "SUBR" is created upon entry to the routine. This variable is *not* the same variable declared in the main program. Indeed, only "SUBR" has access to this variable.

```
B:= (2*fix(U) + 1)/2:

    mark
    link        TOS = REAL, U, acl = r(fix)
    call        fix
    mult        2, fix, TOS
    add         1, tos, TOS
    div         TOS, 2, B
```

The code above does many subtle things. First, a mark is placed on the process (return address) stack. This creates a copy of the registers on the process stack so they can be restored upon returning from the "fix" routine. The "fix" routine can now use the internal registers to execute the body of "fix" and return a value.

The top-of-stack is linked to variable "U" so that the actual parameter "U" is passed via the data stack as a REAL value. This affords type checking between the actual and formal parameters of subprocedure invocation. In this case, "fix" is granted read-only access to the actual parameter, hence the reference is "pass-by-value," and no side effects are allowed.

The "fix" routine is called and a value returned. The product,

$$2 * fix$$

is placed on the top-of-stack by the "mult" instruction which uses 3-address notation:

$$op \quad source, source, destination.$$

Next, the intermediate product is incremented thereby producing another intermediate result on the data stack. Finally, the intermediate data stack result is divided by two (producing a quotient), and stored in variable "B."

```
RETURN  (B)

    copy        B, TOS
    return
end         SUBR;
```

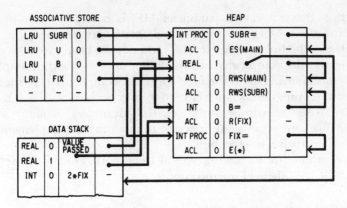

Fig. 9.11 Formal and actual parameter passing.

The resultant value of "B" is copied to the data stack and then the return address is popped from the process stack along with the other registers placed on the process stack by a "mark."

Figure 9.11 shows the state of the system up to the invocation of "fix." First, note the use of the associative memory as a fast symbol table/ page table. The presence bits are all zero indicating that all pages are in main memory.

Second, the heap contains all tagged data needed by "SUBR" during this phase of execution. The most subtle feature is in the mechanism for passing parameters to "fix." Look at entry "U" in the associative store. Follow the reference for "U" into the heap. A REAL tag is located at the reference for "U," and a 1 bit indicating that the value of "U" is to be found somewhere else. Follow the reference pointer next to the 1 bit and locate the actual parameter represented by "U." Remember that "U" was passed by program "MAIN."

The reference pointer for parameter "U" refers to the stack element tagged as a REAL value. Since the main program passed the actual parameter via the stack, the value appears on the stack. However, the access lists must be checked before permitting access to the top-of-stack value.

Follow the acl pointer on the stack. It points to an ACL item in the heap. This item contains an access grant for "SUBR." Therefore, "subr" may access the value passed to it in the name of variable "U." This access list element is identical to the one referenced by formal variable "U," directly.

When formal parameter "U" is passed as the actual parameter "U" in "fix(U)," the following linkage must take place before the actual call to "fix":

link   TOS = REAL, U, acl = r(fix)

Thus, the real valued parameter "U" is passed-by-value to "fix" by linking the top-of-stack to "U" and then restricting access to read-only. Hence, the linkage goes to "U," and not the heap or stack.

Clearly, the complexity of this design approaches the complexity of many programs. This is the idea! Once the complexity is pushed into the hardware, programmers never need to be concerned with it. The programmer "sees" speedcode, only, yet, the advantages of many secure, fast, and low cost systems are inherent in any program implemented in speedcode on such a microcomputer.

We summarize by noting several trends that guided the development of the hypothetical microcomputer.

1. Design with a goal in mind.
2. A multilevel system places complexity at various levels to minimize cost.
3. Memory costs are steadily declining, yet hierarchies are still needed.
4. Processor speed is less valuable than throughput. (Does a "high-level" machine increase throughput?)
5. Protection systems are increasingly more important to total systems design.

The future of microcomputing is great, but limited by the cost and quality of software. If quality systems are to be implemented for the thousands of applications in the future, every opportunity to lessen the programmer's burden must be taken.

Appendix

The following appendix is a reference for the speedcoder. In section A we supply a correspondence with 6800-style kludgecode. Section B is a guide to the 8080 coder, while section C is an index to terms used throughout the book.

A. 6800 Speedcode-to-kludgecode
  i. Basic Actions

Speedcode	Kludgecode
var	RMB, FDB, FBB
const	EQU
identifier	LDAA, STAA PSHA, PULA
arithmetic	ADD A, SUB A, ABA, SBA
Boolean (compares)	CBA, CMP, BEQ, BRA, JMP, BNE, BLT, BGT, BGE

  ii. Choice Action: $\langle\overline{op}\rangle$ is the negative of Boolean $\langle op\rangle$.

if (p $\langle op\rangle$ q)	CMP
	B $\langle op\rangle$ LABEL 2
then	LABEL 1
	.
	.
	.
	BRA END IF
else	LABEL 2
	.
	.
	.
end if	END IF

  iii. Looping Action

while (p $\langle op\rangle$ q) **loop**	LABEL 1
	.
	.
	.
	CMP, CBA
	B $\langle\overline{op}\rangle$ LABEL 2
	.
	.
	.
	BRA LABEL 1
end loop	LABEL 2

  iv. Indexing

A[I]	LDX I
I:= I + 1	INX or DEX

B. 8080 speedcode-to-kludgecode
  i. Basic Actions

Speedcode	Kludgecode
var	
const	
identifier	LDA, PUSH, STA, POP
arithmetic	ADD, SUB
Boolean (comparison)	CMP, CPI, JZ, JMP, JNZ, JM, JP

ii. Choice Action
  if (p ⟨op⟩ q)

                    CMP
                    JZ   ) a compound
                    J $\overline{⟨op⟩}$) Boolean is optional
  then   LABEL 1
                    .
                    .
                    .
                    JMP   END IF
  else   LABEL 2
                    .
                    .
                    .
  end if   END IF

iii. Looping Action
  while (p ⟨op⟩ q) **loop**   LABEL 1
                    .
                    .
                    .
                    CMP
                    J $\overline{⟨op⟩}$ or JZ
                                J $\overline{⟨op⟩}$ LABEL 2
                    .
                    .
                    .
                    JMP LABEL 1
  end loop   LABEL 2

iv. Indexing
  A[I]   LHLD   I
  I:= I + 1   INX H or DCX H

It is sometimes convenient to compare the instruction repertoire of the 6800 with the repertoire of the 8080 microprocessor. This is useful, for instance, when converting a program from one machine to the other. The following list of instructions were used throughout this book.

	8080	:		6800	
General					
LDA	LABEL		LDA	A	LABEL
MVI	A, ohhH	:	LDA	A	#$hh
LDA	LABEL				
MOV	B, A	:	LDA	B	LABEL
STA	LABEL	:	STA	A	LABEL
MOV	A, B				
STA	LABEL		STA	B	LABEL
LXI	SP, immediate	:	LDS		#immediate
CALL	LABEL	:	JSR		LABEL
	RET	:	RTS		
ADD	reg	:	ADDA		LABEL
ADI	immediate				
ADC	reg	:	ADC		

Indexing

LHLD LABEL	:	LDX LABEL
INX H	:	INX
DCX H	:	DEX

Push and Pop always takes two bytes in the 8080!

PUSH PSW (takes condition flags)	:	PSH A; but *not* conditions
POP PSW	:	PUL A
PUSH B	:	PSH B
POP B	:	PUL B

Logical

CMP B	:	CBA
CPI immed.	:	CMP #$hh
JZ LABEL	:	BEQ LABEL
JMP LABEL	:	BRA LABEL
		OR JMP LABEL
JNZ LABEL	:	BNE LABEL
JM LABEL	:	BLT LABEL
JP LABEL	:	BGT LABEL

JZ
JM } BLE

JZ
JP } BGE

Glossary

absolute address   A number that is permanently assigned as the address of a storage location.

access time   The time required to locate a storage location.

accumulator   A register in which the result of an operation is formed.

ACK/NAK   A positive or negative response by a receiving terminal to indicate whether or not a block of data has been received correctly.

acoustic coupler   A form of modem that sends and receives data as tones over a telephone line using a conventional telephone handset.

address   A label, name, or number that designates a location where information is stored.

algorithm   A prescribed set of well-defined rules or processes for the solution of a problem in a finite number of steps.

alphanumeric   Pertaining to a character set that contains both letters and numerals and usually other characters.

argument   (1) A variable or constant that is given in the call of a subroutine as information to it. (2) A variable upon whose value the value of a function depends. (3) The known reference factor necessary to find an item in a table or array (that is, the index).

arithmetic unit   The component of a computer where arithmetic and logical operations are performed.

ARQ   An error control technique in which the receiving station responds with a "NAK" character if a message is received in error. The NAK is interpreted by the sending station as an Automatic Repeat Request.

array   An arrangement of elements into one or more dimensions. A one-dimensional array is commonly called a *vector*; a two-dimensional array is called a *table* or a *matrix*.

ASCII   An abbreviation for American Standard Code for Information Interchange.

ASR   A designation used to indicate the Automatic Send and Receive capabilities of teletypes equipped with punched-tape equipment.

assemble   To translate from a symbolic program to a binary program by substituting binary operation codes for symbolic operation codes and absolute or relocatable addresses for symbolic addresses.

assembler   A program that translates symbolic op-codes into machine language and assigns memory locations for variables and constants.

134

asynchronous transmission   A mode of transmission using start and stop bits to frame a character (hence, frequently called "Start/Stop transmission"). Although bits within a character occur at well-defined intervals, they are not as precisely timed as in synchronous transmission, and characters do not recur at any predictable interval.

atom   The elementary building block of data structures. An atom corresponds to a record in a file and may contain one or more fields of data. Also called *node.*

audio response unit   A unit used in "voice answer back" applications and digitally controlled to produce syllable and word responses to persons entering keyboard data.

auto-indexing   Indexing in which, when addressed indirectly, the content of a location is incremented by one rewritten in the same location and used as the effective address of the current instruction.

autopolling   Performing the polling function automatically to reduce the data communication tasks of the host computer. Autopolling can be performed by communication preprocessors, multiplexors, data concentrators, and the like.

autorestart   A capability of a computer to perform automatically the initialization functions necessary to resume operation following an equipment or power failure.

auxiliary memory   Data storage other than main memory; for example, storage on magnetic tape or direct-access devices.

auxiliary storage   Storage that supplements main memory, such as disk or tape.

average   The statistical mean; the expected value.

average search length   The expected number of comparisons needed to locate an item in a data structure.

backtracking   The operation of scanning a list in reverse.

backward pointer   A pointer which gives the location of an atom's predecessor.

balanced sort   An external tape sort that sorts by merging together tapes, each with an equal number of strings.

bandwidth   A measure of the ability of equipment or transmission links to pass a range of frequencies.

base address   A given address from which an absolute address is derived by combination with a relative address; synonymous with *address constant.*

batch processing   A mode of data processing which processes one job after another in some order.

baud   The maximum rate of transmission of signal elements; usually equivalent to bits per second.

baudot code   A specific code using five bits to represent a character.

BCD code   A specific code using six bits to represent a character, based on the Binary Coded Decimal representation of the decimal digits 0 through 9.

binary   Pertaining to the number system with a radix of two.

binary code   A code that makes use of exactly two distinct characters, 0 and 1.

binary radix sort   A radix sort in which the sort radix is 2.

binary search   A search method which begins with the middle element, discards half the list and repeats on the sublist until a matching key is found or until dividing the list produces an empty list.

binary search tree   A binary search accomplished by storing the list in a binary tree. The tree is ordered when constructed or when insertions are made in order to facilitate the search.

binary tree   A tree in which each node has an outdegree of at most 2.

bit   A unit of information either zero or one (derived from a binary digit).

block   A set of consecutive machine words, characters, or digits handled as a unit, particularly with reference to I/O.

block search   To accomplish a block search, determine the block the item might be in; then linearly search the block.

bootstrap   A technique or device designed to bring a program into the computer from an input device.

BPS   Bits Per Second

branch   A point in a routine where one of two or more choices is made under control of the routine.

break   A communication circuit interruption, frequently used by the receiving terminal to interrupt the transmitting terminal.

broadcast   The transmission of a message intended for all receiving terminals connected to the communication channel.

BROM   Bipolar Read-Only Memory, a read-only memory using large-scale integration (LSI) bipolar devices.

BSC   An IBM designation meaning "Binary Synchronous Communication" and referring to a specific communications procedure using synchronous data transmission.

bubble sort   A sort achieved by exchanging pairs of keys, which begins with the first pair and exchanges successive pairs until the list is ordered; also called *ripple sort*.

buffer   A storage space used to store I/O data temporarily.

buffered I/O   A method of overlapping I/O using two or more buffers.

bug   A mistake in the design or implementation of a program resulting in erroneous results.

byte   A group of binary digits usually operated upon as a unit.

call   To transfer control to a specified routine.

calling sequence   A specified set of instructions and data necessary to set up and call a given routine.

cascade sort   An external tape sort that sorts by merging strings from all but one tape onto the remaining tape. Subsequent passes merge fewer tapes until one tape contains all items.

central processing unit   The unit of a computing system that includes the circuits controlling the interpretation and execution of instructions, that is, the computer proper, excluding I/O and other peripheral devices.

channel, communications   A facility for communicating information; also called a *link, line, circuit, data path*, and the like.

character   A single letter, numeral, or symbol used to represent information.

character checking   The checking of each character by examining all characters as a group or field.

character template   A device used to shape an electron beam into an alphanumeric character for CRT display.

circular list   A linked list in which the last element points to the first one; also called *ring*.

clear   To erase the contents of a storage location by replacing the contents, normally with zeros or spaces; to set to zero.

clear to send   An EIA RS–232–C designation applied to a sense circuit used by a terminal or computer to detect whether its modem is ready to send data.

clock   A device for timing events. In data communications, a clock is required to control the timing of bits sent in a data stream and to control the timing of the sampling of bits received in a data stream.

cluster   *See* Primary cluster; Secondary cluster.

code   A specific relationship between a set of bit patterns and a set of characters.

code level   The number of bits used to represent a character (for example, the five-bit baudot code is a "five-level code").

coding   To write instructions for a computer using symbols meaningful to the computer, or to an assembler, compiler, or other language processor.

collision   An act that occurs when two or more keys hash to the same address.

column-major order   A method of storing a two-dimensional array in which all elements in one column are placed before all elements in the next column. This method can also be used to store higher-dimensional arrays.

command   A user order to a computer system, usually given through a keyboard.

compaction   Packing of data structure to make room in memory.

comparative sort   A sort by comparison of two or more keys.

compatibility   The ability of an instruction or source language to be used on more than one computer.

compile   To produce a binary-coded program from a program written in source (symbolic) language by selecting appropriate subroutines from a subroutine library, as directed by the instructions or other symbols of the source program. The linkage is supplied for combining the subroutines into a workable program, and the subroutine and linkage are translated into binary code.

compiler   A program which translates statements and formulas written in a source language into a machine language program, for example, a FOR-TRAN compiler. Such a program usually generates more than one machine instruction for each statement.

complement   *One's complement:* To replace all 0 bits with 1 bits and vice versa. *Two's complement:* To form the one's complement and add 1.

completeness check   A check that verifies that no fields are missing and that no part of the record has been skipped in sequence.

concatenation   The joining together of two or more strings to form a new one.

conditional assembly   Assembly of certain parts of a symbolic program only if certain conditions have been met.

conditional skip   Transfer of control to another point in the program depending upon whether a condition within the program is met.

connected graph   A graph in which it is possible to get from one node to any other node along a sequence of edges. If the graph is directed, the direction of the edges may be disregarded.

connection matrix   *See* incidence matrix.

consistency check   A check in which two or more pieces of data are considered in relation to each other.

console   Usually the external front side of a device where controls and indicators are available for manual operation of the device.

contiguous data structure   *See* Sequential data structure.

control character   A character inserted into a data stream with the intent of signaling the receiving station to perform some function.

control totals   Totals taken on amount fields or quantity fields of like sizes, such as units, dozens, or cases. These totals are added algebraically.

convert   (1) To change numerical data from one radix to another. (2) To transfer data from one recorded format to another.

count   The successive increase or decrease of a cumulative total of the number of times an event occurs.

counter   A register or storage location (variable) used to represent the number of occurrences of an operation (*see* Loop).

CPS   Characters Per Second

CPU   Central Processing Unit

CRC   A method of error detection using Cyclic Redundancy Check characters. A CRC character, generated at the transmitting terminal, is based on the contents of the message transmitted. A similar CRC generation is performed at the receiving terminal. If the two characters match, the message was probably received correctly.

crossfooting checks   Cross-adding or subtracting two or more fields and zero-balancing the result against the original result. This is an effective control when total debits, total credits, and a balance-forward amount are maintained in each account; total debits and total credits can be crossfooted to prove that the difference equals the balance forward.

CRT   A Cathode Ray Tube used to display information.

current location counter   A counter kept by an assembler to determine the address that has been assigned to either an instruction or constant being assembled.

cursor   A position indicator frequently employed in a display on a video terminal to indicate a character to be corrected or a position in which data is to be entered.

cycle   A path which starts and terminates at the same node.

cycle time   The length of time it takes the computer to reference one word of memory.

cyclic redundancy check   *See* CRC.

cylinder   The tracks of a disk storage device that can be accessed without repositioning the access mechanism.

data   A general term used to denote any or all facts, numbers, letters, and symbols. It connotes basic elements of information which can be processed or produced by a computer.

data modem   A modulation/demodulation device that enables computers and terminals to communicate over telephone circuits.

dataphone   An AT&T designation for a service which provides data communication over telephone facilities.

data set   Another term for *modem*.

data structure   The relationship between data items.

date check   A check the primary purpose of which is to ensure that the record date is acceptable.

DDD   An abbreviation for Direct Distance Dialing, the facility used for making long-distance telephone calls without the assistance of a telephone operator. DDD is frequently used to mean the switched telephone network.

debug   To detect, locate, and correct mistakes in a program.

delimiter   A character that separates, terminates, and organizes elements of a statement or program.

demodulation   A process for deriving information from a modulated carrier.

dense list   A list stored in contiguous locations; also called *linear list, sequential list.*

density   The ratio of the number of information bits to the total number of bits in a structure.

deque   A double-ended queue that allows insertions and deletions at both ends of a list.

device flags   One-bit registers that record the current status of a device.

digit   A character used to represent one of the nonnegative integers smaller than the radix; for example, in binary notation, either 0 or 1.

digital computer   A device that operates on discrete data, performing sequences of arithmetic and logical operations on this data.

digraph   *See* Directed graph.

direct address   An address that specifies the location of an instruction.

directed graph   A set of nodes and edges in which an initial and a terminal node determine the direction of the edge. An edge from node A to node B is not an edge from node B to node A.

directory   A partition by software into several distinct files; a directory of these files is maintained on a device to locate the files.

display register   An internal register in a CRT display terminal.

distributive sort   A sort achieved by partitioning a list and then exchanging items until order exists between partitioned sublists.

division checking   Division is usually checked by multiplication, that is, by multiplying the quotient by the divisor, adding the remainder, and zero-balancing the result against the original dividend.

dope vector   An atom of a linked list that describes the contents of subsequent atoms in the list.

double precision   Pertaining to the use of two computer words to represent one number.

doubly linked list   A linked list in which each atom contains two pointer fields, one of which points to the atom's successor and the other to the atom's predecessor.

dummy   Used as an adjective to indicate an artificial address, instruction, or record of information inserted solely to fulfill prescribed conditions, as in a "dummy" variable.

dump   To copy the contents of all or part of memory, usually onto an external storage medium.

duplex channel   A communication channel with the capability of simultaneous two-way communication; equivalent to *full-duplex.*

dynamic memory management system   A memory system that supplies a variably sized space depending upon the request.

EBCDIC code   A specific code using eight bits to represent a character. The abbreviation stands for Extended Binary Coded Decimal Interchange Code.

echo check   An error control technique wherein the receiving terminal or computer returns the original message to the sender to verify that the message was received correctly.

echo-plex   A communication procedure wherein characters keyboarded by the operator do not print directly on his printer but are sent to a computer that echoes the characters back for printing. This procedure, requiring full-duplex communication facilities, provides a form of error control by displaying to the operator an indication of the character received by the computer.

edge   A connection between two nodes in a graph; it may or may not have direction.

editor   *See* Symbolic editor.

effective address   The address actually used in the execution of a computer instruction.

EIA   Electronic Industries Association.

empty string   A string containing no characters (of length zero); also called *null string*.

EOB   End of Block.

EOM   End of Message.

error control   A plan, implemented by hardware, software, procedures, and the like, to detect and/or correct errors introduced into a data communications system.

error transmission   A change in data resulting from the transmission process.

execute   To carry out an instruction or run a program on the computer.

external fragmentation   Memory loss caused by checkerboarding.

external sort   A sort performed while all or part of a list is stored on an auxiliary storage device.

external storage   A separate facility or device on which data usable by the computer is stored (such as paper tape, magnetic tape, or disk).

fail soft   A method of system implementation designed to prevent the irretrievable loss of facilities or data in the event of a temporary outage of some portion of the system.

field   A unit of information.

field checking   Checking concerned with the contents of fields within records.

FIFO   First In, First Out queue discipline.

file   A collection of related records treated as a unit.

file-structured device   A device such as disk or tape which contains records organized into files and accessible through file names found in a directory file; see Directory.

filename ·   Alphanumeric characters used to identify a particular file.

filename extension   A short appendage to the filename used to identify the type of data in the file; for example, BIN signifying a binary program.

filial set   A collection of "sons" descended from a particular node in a tree.

firmware   That portion of control-memory hardware which can be tailored to create microprograms for a user-oriented instruction set.

fixed point   The position of the radix point of a number system; this position is constant according to a predetermined convention.

flag   A variable or register used to record the status of a program or device; in the latter case, also called a *device flag*.

flip-flop   A device with two stable states.

floating point   A number system in which the position of the radix point is indicated by one part of the number (the *exponent*) and another part represents the significant digits (the *mantissa*).

flowchart   A graphical representation of the operations required to carry out a data processing operation.

forest   A collection of trees.

format   The arrangement of data.

forward pointer   A pointer that tells the location of the next item in a data structure.

four-out-of-eight-code   A communication code which facilitates error detection because four of the eight bits representing a character are always marking.

fragmentation   Loss of usable memory as a result of checkerboarding or mismatch in fit. *See* Internal fragmentation; External fragmentation.

frequency   The rate of recurrence of some cyclic or repetitive event, such as the rate of repetition of a sine-wave electrical current; usually expressed in cycles per second, or Hertz.

frequency division multiplexing   The merging of several signals of lesser bandwidth into a composite signal for transmission over a communication channel of greater bandwidth. Example: five signals with a bandwidth of 100 Hz each might be accommodated on a channel having a bandwidth of 500 Hz.

full duplex   Descriptive of a communications channel capable of simultaneous and independent transmission and reception.

function subprogram   A subprogram that returns a single value result, usually in the accumulator.

garbage collection   Release of unused portions of memory from a data structure to make unused areas of memory available for use.

graph   A set containing two elements: nodes and edges. It provides a mathematical model for data structures in which the nodes correspond to data items and the edges to pointer fields.

half duplex   Descriptive of a communications channel capable of transmission and/or reception, but not both simultaneously.

handshaking   A preliminary procedure performed by modems and/or terminals and computers to verify that communication has been established and can proceed.

hardware   Physical equipment, for example, mechanical, electrical, or electronic devices.

hash totals   A hash total is the sum of the digits of an identifying field.

hashing   A key-to-address transformation in which the keys determine the location of the data.

head   A special data item that points to the beginning of a list. A device that reads or writes data on a storage medium.

header   That part of a message preceding the text, frequently specifying message destination, source, priority, and the like.

heap sort   *See* Tree sort.

hexadecimal system   A numbering system with 16 admissable combinations represented by the symbols 0 through 9 and A through F.

Hollerith code   A specific code using twelve levels of a punched card to represent a character.

horizontal distribution   A method of assigning initial strings to tapes when employing the polyphase sort.

Huffman tree   A minimal value tree; *see* Minimal tree; Optimal merge tree.

incidence matrix   A two-dimensional array that describes the edges in a graph. Also called *connection matrix*.

indegree   The number of directed edges that point to a node.

index   A symbol or numeral that locates the position of an item in an array.

indirect address   An address in a computer instruction that indicates a location where the address of the referenced operand is to be found.

infix notation   A notation where operators are embedded within operands.

initialize   To set counters, switches, and addresses to zero or other starting values at the beginning of, or at prescribed points in, a computer routine.

instruction   A command which causes the computer or system to perform an operation; usually one line of a program.

intelligent terminal   A terminal with some level of programmable "intelligence" for performing preprocessing or postprocessing operations.

interactive   A system that performs processing or problem-solving tasks by carrying on a dialogue with the user.

interface   A well-defined boundary, such as the interface between a modem and a terminal, or the interface between a communications controller and a computer's I/O bus.

internal fragmentation   Memory loss caused by a mismatch between available space and the requested size of space.

internal sort   A sort made while all items remain in main memory.

internal storage   The storage facilities forming an integral physical part of the computer and directly controlled by the computer. Also called main memory and core memory.

interpreter   A program that translates and executes source language statements at run-time.

I/O   Abbreviation for Input/Output.

IRG   Inter-Record Gap.

iteration   Repetition of a group of instructions.

job   A unit of code which solves a problem, that is, a program and all its related subroutines and data.

jump   A departure from the normal sequence of executing instructions in a computer.

K   An abbreviation for the prefix *kilo*, that is, 1024 in decimal notation.

key   One or more fields in a record that is used to locate the record or control its use.

key to address   *See* Hashing.

KSR   A designation used to indicate the Keyboard Send and Printer Receive capabilities of teletypes and comparable equipment.

label   One or more characters used to identify a source language statement or line.

language, assembly   The machine-oriented programming language used by an assembly system.

language, computer   A systematic means of communicating instructions and information to the computer.

language, machine   Information that can be directly processed by the computer; expressed in binary notation.

language, source   A computer language in which programs are first written and which require extensive translation in order to be executed by the computer.

leaf   A terminal node of a tree.

least significant digit   The right-most digit of a number.

level   A measure of the distance from a node to the root of a tree.

library routines   A collection of standard routines which can be incorporated into larger programs.

LIFO   Last In, First Out stack discipline.

limit check   A limit check places upper or lower quantitative limits on a field.

line feed   The teletype operation which advances the paper by one line.

line number   In source languages such as BASIC and FORTRAN, a number which begins a line of the source program for purposes of identification; a numeric label.

linear list   *See* Dense list.

linear search   A search which begins with the first element and compares until a matching key is found or the end of the list is reached.

link   (1) A one-bit register in most computers. (2) An address pointer to the next element of a list or the next record of a file.

linkage   The code that connects two separately coded routines.

linked list   A list in which each atom contains a pointer to the location of the next atom.

list   An ordered collection of atoms.

literal   A symbol which defines itself.

load   To place data or programs into internal storage.

location   A place in storage or memory where a unit of data or an instruction may be stored.

longitudinal redundancy check   A method of error detection using a parity bit for each level in the code being transmitted. Following a block of characters, an LRC character is inserted to make the number of bits transmitted on each of the code levels either odd or even. To check the accuracy of the received data, an LRC character is generated by the receiving terminal and compared with the LRC character received from the transmitting terminal.

loop   A sequence of instructions that is executed repeatedly until a terminal condition prevails.

LRC   Longitudinal Redundancy Check.

machine language programming   This term is used to mean the actual binary machine instructions.

macro instruction   An instruction in a source language that is equivalent to a specified sequence of machine instructions.

main memory   The main high-speed storage of a computer in which binary data is represented by the switching of MOS transistors.

manual input   . The entry of data by hand into a device at the time of processing.

manual operation   The processing of data in a system by direct manual techniques.

mark   The state of a communication channel corresponding to a binary one. The marking condition exists when current flows (hole in paper tape) on a current-loop channel, or when the voltage is more negative than −3 volts on an EIA RS-232-C channel.

mask   A bit pattern which selects those bits from a word of data which are to be used in some subsequent operation.

masking   A technique for sensing specific binary conditions and ignoring others. Typically accomplished by placing zeros in bit positions of no interest, and ones in bit positions to be sensed.

mass storage   Pertaining to a device such as disk or tape which stores large amounts of data readily accessible to the central processing unit.

matrix   A rectangular array of elements; any table can be considered a matrix.

memory   (1) The alterable storage in a computer. (2) Pertaining to a device in which data can be stored and from which it can be retrieved.

memory protection   A method of preventing the contents of some part of main memory from being destroyed or altered.

merge sort   A sort that merges ordered sublists to form a larger ordered list.

message   A group of characters communicated as a unit, typically including a HEADER, TEXT, ERROR CONTROL, and END-OF-MESSAGE indication.

microprogram   A series of microcommands assembled to perform a specific function.

minimal tree   A tree with terminal nodes so placed that the value of the tree is optimal; *see* Optimal merge tree.

modem   A modulation/demodulation device that enables computers and terminals to communicate over telephone circuits.

modulation   A process for impressing information on a carrier.

monitor   The master control program that observes, supervises, controls, or verifies the operation of a system.

most significant digit　The left-most nonzero digit.

multi-drop circuit　A communication system configuration using a single channel or line to serve multiple terminals.

multilinked list　A list in which each atom has two or more pointers.

multiplex　In communications applications, the concurrent transmission of more than one information stream on a single channel.

multiprocessing　Utilization of several computers or processors to divide jobs or processes logically or functionally and to execute them simultaneously.

multiprogramming　Pertains to the execution of two or more programs in main memory at the same time. Execution switches between programs.

nesting　(1) Including a program loop inside another loop. (2) Algebraic nesting, such as $(A+B*(C+D))$, where execution proceeds from the innermost to the outermost level.

network　The interconnection of multiple communication channels and multiple terminals and/or computers.

nil pointer　A pointer used to denote the end of a linked list.

node　*See* Atom.

noise　Signals bearing no desired information and frequently capable of introducing errors into the communication process.

NOP　An instruction that specifically does nothing (control proceeds to the next instruction in the sequence).

normalize　To adjust the exponent and mantissa of a floating-point number so that the mantissa appears in a prescribed format.

null string　A string containing no characters; also called *empty string*.

object program　The binary coded program that constitutes the output after translation of a source language program.

octal　Pertaining to the number system with a radix of 8.

off-line　Pertaining to equipment or devices not under direct control of the computer and to the processes performed on such devices.

on-line　Pertaining to equipment or devices under direct control of the computer and to programs that respond immediately to user commands.

operand　(1) A quantity which is affected, manipulated, or operated upon. (2) The address, or symbolic name, portion of an assembly language instruction.

operating system　A set of programs controlling the operation of a data processing system.

operator　The symbol or code that indicates an action (or operation) to be performed.

optimal merge tree　A tree representation of the order in which strings are to be merged so that a minimum number of move operations occurs.

OR　*Inclusive OR:* A logical operation such that the result is true if either or both operands are true, and false if both operands are false. *Exclusive OR:* A logical operation such that the result is true if either operand is true, and false if both operands are either true or false. When neither case is specifically indicated, inclusive OR is assumed; *see also* Inclusive OR and Exclusive OR.

origin   The absolute address of the beginning of a section of code.

oscillating sort   An external tape sort which capitalizes on a tape drive's ability to read forward and backward. The sort oscillates between an internal sort and an external merge.

outdegree   The number of directed edges leaving a node.

output   Information transferred from the internal storage of a computer to output devices or external storage.

overflow   An act that occurs if the allotted memory for a data structure is exceeded.

pad character   A character inserted to fill a blank time slot in synchronous transmission, or inserted to fulfill a character-count requirement in transmissions of fixed block lengths.

page   A section of main memory.

parallel transmission   The simultaneous transmission of all bits comprising a single character.

parity   A method of error detection using an extra bit to make the total number of marking bits in a character either odd or even. If a character is sent with odd parity, it should be received with odd parity if no errors are introduced by the communication process.

parity check   The examination of a character and its parity bit to determine if the character has been received correctly.

parsing   The process of separating statements into syntactic units.

pass   One complete cycle during which a body of data is processed. An assembler usually requires two passes during which a source program is translated into binary code.

patch   To modify a routine in a rough or expedient way.

path   A path from node n_i to node n_j that is, a set of nodes $n_i, n_{i+1}, \ldots, n_{j-1}, n_j$ and edges such that there is an edge between successive pairs of nodes.

peripheral equipment   In a data processing system, any unit of equipment, distinct from the central processing unit, which may provide the system with outside storage or communication.

pointer   An address or other indication of location.

pointer address   Address of a memory location containing the actual (effective) address of desired data.

polling   The regular and systematic interrogation of terminals to determine if a terminal has messages awaiting transmission, and to determine the state of readiness of a terminal to accept messages.

polyphase sort   An external tape sort which works best with six or fewer tapes. A Fibonacci sequence of merges is established that maintains a maximum number of active tapes throughout the sort.

pop   The act of removing an element from a stack; also called *pull*.

postfix notation   A notation in which operators follow the operands that they operate on.

primary cluster   A buildup of table entries around a single table location.

priority interrupt   An interrupt which is given preference over other interrupts within the system.

procedure   The course of action taken for the solution of a problem; see also *Algorithm*.

program   The complete sequence of instructions and routines necessary to solve a problem.

PROM   Programmable Read-Only Memory; a semiconductor diode array that is programmed by fusing or burning out diode junctions.

protocol   A set of procedures or conventions used routinely between equipment such as terminals and computers.

pseudo-operation   An instruction to the assembler; an operation code that is not part of the computer's hardware command repertoire.

pull   *See* Pop.

push   The act of placing an element on a stack; also called *put.*

pushdown list   A list that is constructed and maintained so that the next item to be retrieved is the item most recently stored in the list.

put   *See* Push.

quadratic quotient search   A hashing algorithm that uses a quadratic offset when probing subsequent table locations.

queue   A list that allows insertion of atoms at one end and deletion of atoms at the opposite end.

queuing   A method of controlling the information processing sequence.

quickersort   A sort performed by partitioning a list into two sublists and a pivotal middle element. All items greater than the pivot go in one sublist and all lesser items go in the other sublist. Sublists are further subdivided until all items are ordered.

radix   The base of a number system; the number of digit symbols required by a number system.

radix sort   A distributive sort that uses a number of partitions equal to the sort radix.

random access   A method of retrieving data from a secondary storage device in which the retrieval time is independent of the location of the data; contrast with Sequential access.

range check   A range check is usually applied to a code in order to verify that it falls within a given set of characters or numbers.

read   To transfer information from an input device to memory.

real-time   Pertaining to a computation performed while the related physical process is taking place so that results of the computation can be used in guiding the physical process.

reasonableness check   A programmed judgment on data to determine whether it is normal.

record   A collection of related data items (a collection of related records makes up a *file.*

recursion   A reactivation of an active process; for example, a program segment which calls itself.

recursive subroutine   A subroutine capable of calling itself.

redundancy   A repetition of information or the insertion of information which is not new, and therefore redundant. Example: the use of check bits and check characters in data communication is a form of redundancy; hence the terms: cyclic redundancy, longitudinal redundancy, vertical redundancy.

redundancy check   The use of redundancy to check errors; *see* CRC, LRC, VRC.

register   A device capable of storing a specified amount of data, usually one word.

relative address   The number that specifies the difference between the actual address and a base address.

relocatable   Descriptive of a routine whose instructions are written so that they can be located and executed in different parts of main memory.

remote   Physically distant from a local computer, terminal, multiplexor, and the like.

replacement-selection   A tournament method of sorting tape files that produces ordered strings of various lengths which must be merged.

response time   Time between initiating an operation from a remote terminal and obtaining the result (including transmission time to and from the computer, processing time, and access time for the files employed).

restart   To resume execution of a program.

ring   *See* Circular list.

ripple sort   *See* Bubble sort.

RJE   An IBM designation meaning Remote Job Entry and referring to the programs used to submit processing jobs from terminals.

RO   A designation used to indicate the Receive Only capabilities of teletypes and other equipment lacking keyboards and paper-tape equipment.

ROM   A Read Only Memory system wherein the stored bit patterns cannot be rewritten or otherwise altered.

root   The node with indegree zero.

routine   A set of instructions arranged in proper sequence so that the computer can perform a desired task; a program or subprogram.

row-major order   A method of storing a two-dimensional array in which all elements in one row are placed before all elements in the next row; *see also* Column-major order.

RS–232   A technical specification published by the Electronic Industries Association establishing the interface requirements between modems and terminals or computers.

run   A single, continuous execution of a program.

scan   An algorithmic procedure for visiting or listing each node of a data structure.

scatter storage   *See* Hashing.

secondary cluster   A build-up along a path established by a pattern in a hashing function used for table look-up.

segment   (1) That part of a long program which may be resident in main memory at any one time. (2) To divide a program into two or more segments or to store part of a routine on an external storage device so that it may be brought into main memory as needed.

selection sort   A sort that selects the extreme value (largest or smallest) in a list, exchanges it with the last value in the list, and repeats with a shorter list.

self-checking number   A self-checking number is one that has a precalculated digit appended to the basic number for the purpose of catching keypunch or transmission errors.

sequence check   A check performed if incoming data records must be sequenced for further processing. If applicable, this type of check can be expanded to include a check on multiple records making up one transaction.

sequential access   An access method for storing or retrieving data items which are located in a continuous manner. The retrieval time of an item depends in part on how many items precede it.

sequential data structure   A data structure in which each atom is immediately adjacent to the next atom; also called *contiguous data structure*.

sequential list   *See* Dense list.

sequential search   *See* Linear search.

serial access   Pertaining to the sequential or consecutive transmission of data to or from memory, as with paper tape; contrast with Random access.

serial transmission   The transmission of the bits of a character in sequence, one at a time.

shift   A movement of bits to the left or right that is frequently performed in the accumulator.

simplex   Communication in only one direction.

simulate   To represent the function of a device, system, or program with another device, system, or program.

single step   Operation of a computer in such a manner that only one instruction is executed each time that the computer is started.

software   The collection of programs and routines associated with a computer.

sort   The process of placing a list in order; *see* Binary radix sort, Bubble sort, Comparative sort, Distributive sort, External sort, Internal sort, Merge sort, Quickersort, Radix sort, Selection sort, Tree sort.

sort effort   The number of comparisons or moves needed to order an unordered list.

source language   *See* Language, source.

source program   A computer program written in a source language.

space   The state of a communication channel corresponding to a binary zero. The spacing condition exists when no current flows (no hole in paper tape) on a current-loop channel, or when the voltage is more positive that +3 volts on an EIA RS–232–C channel.

spanning tree   A subgraph of a graph with two properties: First, it is a tree, and second, it contains all the nodes of the original graph.

sparse array   An array in which most of the entries have a value of zero.

stack   A list that restricts insertions and deletions to one end.

start bit   A bit used in asynchronous transmission to precede the first bit of a character transmitted serially, signaling the start of the character.

statement   An expression or instruction in a source language.

stop bit   A bit (or bits) used in asynchronous transmission to signal the end of a character transmitted serially, and representing the quiescent state in which the line will remain until the next character begins.

stop code   A control character which, in the case of a teletype, turns off the paper tape reader.

storage allocation   The assignment of blocks of data and instructions to specified blocks of storage.

storage capacity   The amount of data that can be contained in a storage device.

storage device　A device in which data can be entered, retained, and retrieved.

store　To enter data into a storage device.

string　A series of characters stored in a contiguous area in memory.

structure　The organization or arrangement of the parts of an entity.

subroutine, closed　A subroutine not stored in the main part of a program; such a subroutine is normally called or entered with a branch instruction, and provision is made to return control to the main routine at the end of the subroutine.

subroutine, open　A subroutine that must be relocated and inserted into a routine at each place it is used.

subscript　One of a set of characters used to index the location of item in an array.

swapping　In a time-sharing environment, the action of either temporarily bringing a user program into main memory or storing it on a system device.

switch　A device or programming technique for making selections.

symbol table　A table in which symbols and their corresponding values are recorded.

symbolic address　A set of characters used to specify a memory location within a program.

symbolic editor　A system program which helps users in the preparation and modification of source language programs by adding, changing, or deleting lines of text.

sync character　A character transmitted to establish character synchronization in synchronous communication. When the receiving station recognizes the sync character, the receiving station is said to be synchronized with the transmitting station, and communication can begin.

synchronous transmission　A mode of transmission using that synchronizes a character stream with a time bit stream.

synonym　Two or more keys that produce the same table address when hashed.

system　A combination of software and hardware that performs specific processing operations.

table　A collection of data stored for ease of reference, usually as an array.

tail　A special data item that locates the end of a list.

tariff　A published schedule of regulated charges for common carrier services and equipment.

teleprinter　An automatic printing device operated by electrically coded signals from a keyboard.

teleprocessing system　Data processing equipment used in combination with terminal equipment and communication facilities.

teletype　Any of several configurations of keyboards, printers, and paper-tape equipment manufactured by the Teletype Corporation.

telpak　A type of communication link provided by common carriers that represents a band of frequencies which can be subdivided into voice and data channels of various bandwidths.

temporary storage　Storage locations reserved for immediate results.

terminal　A peripheral device in a system through which data can enter or leave the computer.

terminal node   A node of a tree which has no successors.

test for alphabetic   A check that guarantees correct alphabetic input.

test for blanks   In this test, an indication must be made as to which fields must be blank. If the field requires blanks, a constant of the proper number of blanks is compared against the field, and a test made for an equal condition. An unequal comparison indicates an error condition.

test for numeric   A test of a numeric field to ensure against its having interspersed blanks and/or extraneous zone bits. Blanks are replaced by zeros. If the numeric field may not contain zone bits, zones are stripped from the field by the appropriate instructions.

test for sign   A check made to ensure that the proper algebraic sign is present for the type of transaction involved.

text editor   A program that assists in the preparation of text.

threaded tree   A tree containing additional pointers to assist in the scan of the tree.

time division multiplexing   The merging of several bit streams of lower bit rates into a composite signal for transmission over a communication channel of higher bit-rate capacity. Example: five bit streams operating at 100 bps might be accommodated on a channel having a capacity of 500 bps. Combining the data streams is accomplished by assigning a "time-slice" of the high-speed channel to each of the low-speed channels.

time quantum   In time-sharing, a unit of time allotted to each user by the monitor.

timesharing   A method of allocating central processor time and other computer resources to multiple users so that the computer, in effect, apparently processes a number of programs simultaneously.

toggle   To use switches to enter data into the computer memory.

token   A code or symbol representing a name or entity in a programming language.

track   The portion of a magnetic storage medium which passes under a positioned read/write head.

traffic intensity   The ratio of insertion rate to the deletion rate of a queue.

transducer   A device that converts information in one form into information in another form.

translate   To convert from one language to another.

tree   A connected graph with no cycles. A *directed tree* is a directed graph that contains no cycles and no alternate paths; it has a unique node (the root) whose successor set consists of all the other nodes.

tree sort   A sort that exchanges items treated as nodes of a tree. When an item reaches the root node, it is exchanged with the lowest leaf node. (Also called *heap sort*.).

truncation   The reduction of precision by dropping one or more of the least significant digits; for example, 3.141592 truncated to four decimal digits is 3.141.

unattended operation   Transmission and/or reception without an operator.

underflow   An act that occurs when an attempt is made to access an item in a data structure that contains no items; contrast with Overflow.

update   A method to modify a master file with current information, according to a specified procedure.

USASCII   An abbreviation for United States of America Standard Code for Information Interchange, a specific code using seven bits to represent a character.

user   Programmer or operator of a computer.

variable   A symbol whose value changes during the execution of a program.

vector   In computer science, a data structure that permits the location of any item by the use of a single index or subscript; contrast with a table, or matrix, which requires two subscripts to locate an item uniquely.

voice-grade channel   Typically, a telephone circuit used for speech communication and accommodating frequencies from 300 to 3,000 Hz.

VRC   Vertical Redundancy Check (*see* Parity).

white noise   Noise (electrical or acoustical) whose energy spectrum is uniformly distributed across all frequencies within a band of interest.

wideband channel   A communication channel having a bandwidth greater than that of a voice-grade line and usually some multiple of the bandwidth of a voice-grade line.

word   A unit of data that may be stored in one addressable location.

WPM   Words Per Minute; a measure of transmission speed.

wrap data   The transmission of data through a communications system and the return of the data to its source to test the accuracy of the system.

write   To transfer information from main memory to a peripheral device or to auxiliary storage.

Index

Index